MURIEL SPARK

LITERATURE AND LIFE SERIES
[Formerly Modern Literature and World Dramatists]

Selected list of titles:

Complete list of titles in the series available from publisher on request.

MURIEL SPARK

Velma Bourgeois Richmond

Frederick Ungar Publishing Co. / New York

Library of Congress Cataloging in Publication Data

Richmond, Velma Bourgeois.
  Muriel Spark.

  (Literature and life series)
  Bibliography: p.
  Includes index.
  1. Spark, Muriel—Criticism and interpretation.
I. Title. II. Series.
PR6037.P29Z88 1984   823'.914   82-40267
ISBN 0-8044-2731-3

Acknowledgments

Several people have graciously supported me in the writing of this book. The staff of the British Library were especially helpful in providing magazines and newspapers. My husband, Hugh Richmond, and our daughters, Elizabeth and Claire, were understanding when my time was given to writing rather than other activities, particularly during a summer in Italy. Two acknowledgments about reprinting are appropriate: Chapter 8 is a revised version of an article I published as "The Darkening Vision of Muriel Spark," in *Critique*, XV (1973), pp. 71–85. The quotation from Muriel Spark's poetry, "Against the Transcendentalists," Copyright 1952 by Copyright Administration Limited, is reprinted by permission.

Velma Bourgeois Richmond

In memory of
Isabel and Ronald Richmond,
inspirers of my love for Scotland

Acknowledgments

Contents

Chronology

1918 Muriel Sarah Camberg was born in Edinburgh, Scotland, on February 1, 1918.

1938 Muriel married S. O. Spark in Rhodesia. (She had one son, Robin, and the marriage was dissolved.)

1944 Muriel Spark returned to England and worked in the Political Intelligence Office during World War II.

1947–49 Muriel Spark edited *The Poetry Review* in London.

1951 The first effort at fiction, "The Seraph and the Zambesi," won *The Observer* Christmas story competition.

1952 Muriel Spark published a volume of poems, *The Fanfarlo and Other Verse*. In the early 1950s, she also published several critical books and editions of nineteenth-century English writers—William Wordsworth, Mary Wollstonecraft Shelley, Emily Brontë—some in collaboration.

1954 Muriel Spark converted to Roman Catholicism.

1957 Her first novel, *The Comforters*, was published, as well as *The Letters of John Henry Newman* (edited with Derek Stanford).

1959 Her third novel, *Memento Mori*, was a critical and financial success.

1961 Muriel Spark gained wealth and fame with *The Prime of Miss Jean Brodie*, a great popular success.

1965 Spark went to live in New York. She also published her longest novel, *The Mandelbaum Gate*, which won the James Tait Black Memorial Prize.

1967 Spark received the Order of the British Empire, published *Collected Stories I* and *Collected Poems I*, and moved to Rome.

1970 *The Driver's Seat*, Spark's tenth novel, showed a shift to sharper satirical ridicule and unrelieved harshness.

1

About Muriel Spark

A prolific and very popular writer, Muriel Spark is known not only for her novels but also for her dramatic pieces. She has been described as brilliant but also disappointing and perhaps most frequently as puzzling. Her interviews as well as her fiction reveal some uncertainty and ambiguity. She is outrageously playful even about serious subjects that are important to her. Her most distinctive quality is a detachment that reflects both deep concern for truth and relentless humor. Unlike most satirists who explore foibles by a focus on the world, Spark always combines analysis with a perspective rooted in the spiritual world. Her biography and critical statements about the art of fiction contribute to an understanding and evaluation of her achievement.

Muriel Sarah was born on February 1, 1918, in Edinburgh. Her engineer father, Bernard Camberg, was a Jew, a rather simple religious man. Her English mother, Elizabeth Maud Uezzell, was more sophisticated, rather flamboyant, fascinated by the arts, and a lover of elegance. Spark's grandmother kept a small shop in Watford, near London, and was remarkably independent; she championed women's suffrage and was devoted to social improvement. These three were Spark's most important family influences during the first eighteen years of her life, which she spent in the Scottish capital.

With characteristic wit, precision, and imagination, Muriel Spark wrote in 1975 a piece about "The First Year of My Life," a time during which she never smiled.[1] In the piece, she depicted herself as a baby able to know everything going on in the world, and the last year of World War I was not a happy time. The best and strongest young men were killed on the Western Front; in Russia there was revolution and the murder of the Romanoff family; and dubious leaders pontificated in Britain. Mr. Asquith made a platitudinous declaration to the House of Commons that "the war had cleansed and purged the world, so that it was a privilege to play a part." Baby Muriel responded with a decided smile. Subsequently, she insisted, "When I really mean a smile, deeply felt from the core," it comes from this experience of the absurdity of human pretention and lack of understanding. These are Muriel Spark's subject matter, and her perspective remains coolly detached and ironic.

In Edinburgh Muriel attended James Gillespie's Girls' School, which became the model for Marcia Blaine's School in *The Prime of Miss Jean Brodie*, her most famous work. She was "the school's Poet and Dreamer, with appropriate perquisites and concessions."[2] Her early view of herself as an artist was much revised by her experiences in the world where art is not so highly valued, and one of her frequent interests in her early novels is the nature of art and of artistic temperament. Edinburgh's greatest novelist, Sir Walter Scott, enormously influenced the nineteenth century by presenting a Romantic view of life, and Spark was fascinated by the attractions of this view. Nevertheless, the opposite, satiric observation, prevailed in her work with increasing intensity.

In "What Images Return," she wrote of her early years:

Edinburgh is the place that I, a constitutional exile, am essentially exiled from. . . . It was Edinburgh that bred within me the conditions of exiledom; and what have I been doing since then but moving from exile into exile? It has ceased to be a fate, it has become a calling.

In the same essay, she provided additional insights about those early years by identifying the word "nevertheless" as "the core of a thought pattern" with Edinburgh. Spark claimed that she was "fairly indoctrinated" by this habit of thought and made decisions accordingly. In addition, she derived from Edinburgh a "puritanical strain" and "haughty and remote anarchism," a lack of confidence in politics and politicians, and a sense of time from pre-history to the present.

Spark's first exile epitomized such contrasts, for in 1937 she went from Scotland to Rhodesia, a bright and hot land. She married S. O. Spark in 1938, had one son, Robin, but was soon divorced. At least one detail from this experience, a husband shooting his wife in the foot, appeared in a short story entitled "Bang Bang You're Dead." Although all were written much later, some of her best short stories, like "The Go-Away Bird" and "The Portobello Road," used African subjects.

In 1944 Spark returned to England to work in the Political Intelligence Department of the British Foreign Office under very secret conditions at Woburn Abbey, London. Part of her work, distorting news to lower German morale, was an early experience of creating fiction. This activity was later used in *The Hothouse by the East River*. To paraphrase her later criticism, she told lies to arrive at a higher truth. She remained in London after the war and supported herself as a journalist, while trying to establish herself as a poet. In 1947 she became General-Secretary of the

Poetry Society; she edited *The Poetry Review* until 1949.

Spark's early literary career was dedicated to poetry. She published *The Fanfarlo and Other Verse* in 1952, and she encouraged other poets. But she was also an active critic, a frequent contributor to periodicals, occasionally using the pseudonym Evelyn Cavallo. Her books of criticism included studies of Mary Shelley and John Masefield, and she also edited collections of the poems of Emily Brontë and of the Brontë letters. These subjects provided intense exposure to Romantic literature. With her collaborator Derek Stanford, she edited the letters of John Henry Newman and of Mary Shelley and essays about Wordsworth; they also coauthored a study of Emily Brontë. Stanford's critical and biographical study of Muriel Spark provides the fullest account of these London years and is the first book written about her. There has been no such biography for the period of her major career.

Spark's first attempt to write fiction, "The Seraph and the Zambesi," won *The Observer*'s Christmas short-story competition in 1951. This led to an invitation from Macmillan to produce a novel, and Spark's career as a writer of fiction was launched. She has never stopped publishing poems, and in "The House of Fiction" interview of 1970 she insisted: "I think I am still a poet. I think my novels are the novels of a poet. I think like a poet and react as one."[3] The British critic Frank Kermode early called her a "poet-novelist," and others have accepted this description.

The change to prose as her chief form was a consequence of Spark's choice of reading in these years. In "My Conversion" she named three writers who profoundly influenced her—Marcel Proust, John Henry Newman, and Max Beerbohm.[4] To some this seemed a bizarre combination, but Spark reiterated her point in

"Writers in the Tense Present."[5] These authors were
clearly reflected in her writing.[6]

Beerbohm was a favorite author, for two or three
years, beginning in 1949. This polished stylist inspired
Spark to create "subtle English prose with the shorter
words the better and a nice witty turn to it all." Her
early stories reflected both this distinctive manner and
tone of nonchalant impertinence.

Proust, as the author of *A la recherche du temps
perdu*, has had enormous impact upon the modern
novel. Spark read him in Scott-Moncrieff's translation,
and his work was very important to her in several
ways. In an article called "The Religion of an
Agnostic," she described him as an economical writer
(for all his twelve volumes) and one who stimulated
her creativity. Most significant was Proust's withdrawal from society, at the age of thirty-six, "to contemplate its inner decadence and to whom those very
symbols of decay yielded their permanent essence,
restored in eternity." She saw in Proust an ironic acceptance of the fact that "the most unlikely people,
places and things are shown as the repositories of invisible grace."[7]

Certainly Proust and Beerbohm were significant,
but Newman was probably most crucial. Spark has
said that he was "a tremendous influence." During the
1950s, she read deeply and was early attracted to
Newman's statement that a Christian view of the
universe is a poetic one, but she did not immediately
embrace Catholicism. She found many of the
Catholics she met far less appealing than the lucid
prose and steady spiritual development of the great
nineteenth-century theologian. She became an Anglo-
Catholic in 1953, and for a time attended T.S. Eliot's
church, St. Stephen's, before her conversion to Roman
Catholicism in 1954. Like Newman, Spark moved
gradually from low church to Rome. Derek Stanford

described her at this time as a pilgrim figure, dressed
in green, striding through Hertfordshire, discussing
religion with friends, and receiving instructions from a
Benedictine.

The crucial instruction, however, came from
Newman's writing. In her critical discussion of
"Newman as a Catholic" in the *Letters*, she stressed
the consistency in Newman's fundamental development, while noting that his writings were not "a neat
and rounded whole." She described Newman as "a
social exile" and quoted a passage from his journal in
which he contrasted his present situation with being a
Protestant: "As a Protestant, I felt my religion dreary,
but not my life—but, as a Catholic, my life dreary,
not my religion." Spark noted the frequent journal entries about depression and Newman's inevitable
isolation because of his temperament and intellectual
superiority and originality. She concluded the
discussion by recognizing that England's great Cardinal had little sympathy from persons within the
Catholic Church but derived "full satisfaction in its
creed, theology, rites, sacraments, discipline, *a
freedom yet a support also.*" Her interest in Newman
was of long duration, as was explicitly demonstrated
in *Loitering with Intent*, her autobiographical novel
of 1981.

Cardinal Newman was an author who shaped
Muriel Spark in many ways. His graceful prose and the
conversational quality of his writing helped her at a
time when she was moving from poetry to prose. His
situation as an "exile" corresponded to her own experiences. The isolation that came from Newman's
superior gifts paralleled Spark's circumstance of
needing constantly to move on to a new situation once
she had mastered the old. Derek Stanford saw two
recurring patterns in her life—"appropriation" and
"saturation," followed by dismissal. Further,
Newman's thought suggested answers to fundamental

questions. Living in an age of rapidly evolving materialism, Newman wrote frequently about his "mistrust in the reality of material phenomena." He also had much to say about self-knowledge, stressing the heart as well as the mind, and he argued always the limits of human comprehension, the necessity for faith that goes beyond reason. Significantly, he provided the most severe challenge when he observed the difficulty of the modern world: "Christianity has never yet had the experience of a world simply irreligious." To achieve and to communicate a sense of belief in such a world was a fit task for a writer who was taking a long time to find her way.

Muriel Spark's conversion is the single most important fact in her life, for it made possible her ordering of experience and her resultant shaping as a writer. Recent Roman Catholic converts were frequent protagonists in her early novels, and Spark has been described as a Catholic novelist—often by very uneasy Catholics. It is, then, necessary to define the conversion not simply in religious but in intellectual terms. As a coherent way of looking at the universe, "an economical system because all the blank spaces are filled in," Roman Catholicism provided Muriel Spark with the structure she needed. The intellectual advantages of being in a system, in contrast to moving aimlessly in a less precisely governed, "freer" world of moral relativity, are what made the difference for Spark:

I'm quite certain that my conversion gave me something to work on as a satirist. The Catholic belief is a norm from which one can depart. It's not a fluctuating thing. I'm not advocating the Catholic Faith as this for everyone, but for me, it's provided my norm. The Catholic Church for me is just a formal declaration of what I believe in any case. It's something to measure from. But I never think of myself as a Catholic when I'm writing because it's so difficult to think of myself as anything else. It's all instinctive. This obviously affects the characters I write about and the way I see life in my books.[8]

In 1955, with encouragement and an advance from Macmillan, Spark began her first novel, *The Comforters*. She went to Aylesford to live in a tiny cottage owned by the Carmelite Friary. She named it "St. Jude's Cottage," after the patron saint of hopeless causes, a pointed and rueful choice. At this time she was under considerable nervous strain, having experienced hallucinations. During this period she also received generous support from a variety of literary people and was helped by therapy to regain her health. The novel was published in 1957 and immediately received widespread praise. In this first sustained effort, she introduced what were to become familiar characteristics—a loner heroine who is a recent convert to Roman Catholicism and a writer, mysterious narrative circumstances, sharp satirical analysis of character and situation, experiences that go beyond the material world, surprise twists in plotting, witty dialogue, convincing conversational manner, and unexpected conclusions.

A fundamental artistic question was also raised, for as Spark explained in "The House of Fiction" interview,

> I was asked to write a novel, and I didn't think much of novels. I thought it was an inferior way of writing. So I wrote a novel to work out the technique first, to sort of make it all right with myself to write a novel at all—a novel about writing a novel.[9]

In *The Comforters* those who write novels are seen as "professional liars," just as in the later novel *Memento Mori*, the art of writers of fiction is described as "very like the practice of deception." Recognition of this view is fundamental to an understanding of Spark's fiction, for it explains how to interpret her extraordinary vision, which can otherwise seem merely willful and indulgent.

Spark further explained exactly how she intended her novels to be regarded:

> I don't claim that my novels are truth—I claim that they are fiction, out of which a kind of truth emerges. And I keep in mind specifically that what I am writing is fiction because I am interested in truth—absolute truth—and I don't pretend that what I'm writing is more than an imaginative extension of the truth—something inventive. . . . There is metaphorical truth and moral truth, and what they call anagogical truth, you know, the different sorts of truth, and there is absolute truth, in which I believe things which are difficult to believe, but I believe them because they are absolute. And this is one aspect of truth perhaps. But in fact if we are going to live in the world as reasonable beings, we must call it lies. But simply because we put it out as a work of fiction, then one is not a liar.[10]

After her first major work of fiction, Spark continued to publish at a startling rate, a book almost every year. She described her process of composition as a long time of thinking about the idea, often with an obsessive concentration that ignored everything else, and then a period of about eight weeks devoted to the actual writing of the novel. Most of the novels are short, and though the Sparkian manner was unmistakable, their variety is remarkable as is their fluency. An interviewer explained that Spark wrote neatly in school exercise books, each with seventy-two pages that equal 10,000 words.[11] Spark's insistence upon the "economical" appeared here too.

After a second novel and a collection of short stories, Spark published in 1959 a masterpiece, *Memento Mori*. One of the remarkable achievements of twentieth-century fiction, it remains for many her most "satisfying" book.[12] Her apprenticeship was clearly ended, for here was an expansion from a single

protagonist to a complex group of characters and a
freeing from the subjective "I" that had marred her
second novel, *Robinson*. The handling of suspense
suggested Spark's indebtedness to mystery writers like
Agatha Christie and Josephine Tey. The deaths, including a violent murder, were less important than understanding the message, "Remember you must die."
Each person hears it, but the voice differs. This novel
is solidly based on religious understanding. Its purpose
is to make clear in modern references, as had the
traditional medieval morality play *Everyman*, the
necessity for recognizing the limits of the material
world and the absurdity of thinking one will not die,
and of perpetuating foolish human desires.

The next year two novels were published, both set in
London where Spark was still living. *The Ballad of
Peckham Rye*, she explained, was written "to give her
mind a holiday and to write something light and
lyrical."[13] *The Bachelors* was more serious; it is an
early investigation of the idea of community—a
recurring theme in Spark's work. The peculiarly twentieth-century malaise, solipsism—that unwillingness
to transcend selfish concerns—steadily increased in the
1960s, and Spark intensified her ridicule of it in later
novels.

After three novels that avoided concentration upon
the female heroine, Muriel Spark began another group
of novels that Peter Kemp described as "the most self-
contained   and   tightly   knit   unit,   advancing
chronologically through thirty years of this century
and linked by a chain of historical reaction . . . and
having an obvious debt to autobiography."[14] The first
also changed Muriel Spark's situation as an author.
Though her work had been sufficiently widely
recognized to result in her inclusion in *Who's Who
1961*, it was the appearance in that year of *The Prime
of Miss Jean Brodie* that brought international fame
and wealth.

First published in *The New Yorker*, this short novel
was set in Edinburgh in the 1930s, the time when
Spark was a schoolgirl. Its economical fusion of personal, political, and moral concerns, as well as the
charismatic character of the teacher, its deliciously
witty style, and its hilarious literary parodies, have all
made it the most widely read and best known of
Spark's novels. Through adaptations for theater, film,
and television, it reached an even wider audience. In
The Prime of Miss Jean Brodie, Spark goes further in
investigating the moral nature of man, through a subtle doubling and counterpointing of the teacher Miss
Brodie and her notable pupil Sandy Stranger, who
becomes a Catholic nun and writes a psychological
study of "The Transfiguration of the Commonplace"—a title frequently used by critics to
describe Muriel Spark's brilliance.

Her reputation was also enlarged in 1961 through
the publication of *Voices at Play*, a collection of short
stories and radio plays that had been broadcast by the
BBC on "The Third Programme." In the preface Spark
explained that both plays and stories "were very much
affected by each other," and that it was "by accident"
that each turned out in its particular form.

A full-length play, *Doctors of Philosophy*, presented
in 1963, was highly experimental and not very successful. It examined illusions of the theater in ways
analogous to Spark's questioning of the novel as a
form, for she shifted the laws of the theater to look at
reality as it is perceived in the world. More widely ac-
claimed that year was *The Girls of Slender Means*.
Here Spark was back in her familiar London setting
and again presented a specialized community, young
women living at the May of Teck Club at the end of
World War II. Her tone was lighter, but concern for
the moral universe remained. Conversion to Roman
Catholicism was again the significant event. This

time, however, the means were altered, for, with
Nicholas Farrington, "a vision of evil was as effective
to conversion as a vision of good."

After seven novels and two collections of stories in
seven years, Muriel Spark did not publish a novel for
two years. Then came *The Mandelbaum Gate*. Un-
characteristically long and on a much larger scale than
anything else she had written, it was quite different in
style. The heroine Barbara Vaughan was more richly
developed than any other; the setting in Jerusalem was
both exotic in realistic terms and more significant symbolically. The theme was enormous ("Everything's a
subject for a Christian pilgrimage if you widen the
scope enough"), and the resolutions positive. Spark explained in an interview that it was an extremely important book for her, the one that took the most effort.[15] Certainly she has never written another like it,
and it has been hard for critics to place.

After 1965, there were many major shifts in Spark's
work. She was no longer living in London but in New
York, in an apartment near the United Nations
Building. This was another exile, and in a culture
divorced from the British tradition. Further, the 1960s
were a time of unrest, protest, and disillusionment
throughout the Western world. Spark's career as a
writer of fiction was directly related to her conversion
to Roman Catholicism, and the Church, through the
Vatican Councils and their implementation, was un-
dergoing changes, many of which sharply modified
the firm tradition that had been so attractive and sup-
portive. In addition, after living in modest circumstances for years, she now found herself rich.

In 1967, she moved from the capital of the modern
world to that of the ancient, Rome. Spark redefined
her role as an artist when she addressed the American
Academy of Arts and Letters in 1971 and argued that
only "the art of ridicule can penetrate to the
marrow."[16] In the present world of absurdity, only the
severest challenge, the uncomfortable mental stimu-

lation that leaves people uneasy rather than complacent, can be effective.

Collected Poems I and *Collected Stories I* were
published in 1967, the year that Spark also received
the Order of the British Empire for artistic
achievement. Like *The Mandelbaum Gate*, these
marked the end of the first major phase of her work.
The next novel, *The Public Image*, was published in
1968 and provided a transition. The setting is Rome.
The artistic figure was a film star, Annabel
Christopher, a performer whose real person bears little
relation to her publicized role as English Lady-Tiger.
The novel shows the enthusiasm for cult personalities
and the hedonism that were typical of the 1960s, but
the conclusion is positive, because the heroine abandons the public image to concentrate upon inner
resources and her baby, thus rejecting the blan-
dishments of mere materialism.

The next two novels were much less reassuring.
They presented a darkening vision expressed through
tales of horror and murder, told in the present tense to
create a sense of immediacy. *The Driver's Seat* (1970)
and *Not to Disturb* (1971) show two opposites of
behavior—an assumption of absolute control of experience, of playing God, and a refusal to become involved, "doing one's thing" only. But the two novels
were alike in a cold representation of bizarre action
mingled with ruthless ridicule of the characters who
have no idea that man is a moral creature.

There was again a period of two years between
novels, and *The Hothouse by the East River*, published
in 1973, showed new directions. Here the physical setting was New York and the anagogic place was
purgatory. With a greater variety of theme and a shifting in tone, the novel has a largeness reminiscent of
The Mandelbaum Gate. Just as that novel and
Memento Mori were followed by lighter short novels,
so *The Hothouse by the East River* was succeeded by

The Abbess of Crewe. Written in six weeks, a hilarious spoof of the Watergate scandal and coverup corruption that led to the resignation of President Richard Nixon, this novel disconcerted many. There was, of course, a serious intention: the choice of setting, an abbey, allowed Spark to ridicule the sweeping changes that have occurred in the outlook of many Catholics since Vatican II—for example, modernist ideas of religion as social consciousness and confusions about human sexuality. After two dark novels, this one was light in tone, but through the hilarity there was a provocative questioning.

A somewhat genial attitude survived in *The Takeover,* which is set in Italy, where kidnapping, theft, and murder among the very rich increase steadily. The need for something beyond the limits of the material world was reiterated by showing how completely unreliable are its wealth and security. Obvious ridicule was of trendy exploiters of ecological concerns and the hectic search for cults—here the restoration of an ancient religion—that characterized the 1970s.

The increasing diffuseness mirrored in the people and world described in *The Takeover* is heightened in *Territorial Rights.* The setting is Venice; the characters are international; and the actions are betrayals, murder, kidnapping, blackmail, theft. Techniques of the thriller are interlaced liberally with the absurdity and peculiarity of human behavior. Nevertheless, *Territorial Rights* expands thematically to explore evil, defined as the absence of good. Evil, here seen in total disregard of others, is recognized as something enjoyed by those who are wrongdoers.

Spark's next novel, *Loitering with Intent,* is an autobiographical exploration and explanation of the life of the artist. Reflection as the mature and successful writer of fiction reaffirmed Spark's early admiration of John Henry Newman. His autobiography,

along with that of Benvenuto Cellini, has a major influence in this book. Together the two represent the
complementary spiritual and material being. Richly
presented are many details of how Spark works as a
writer and investigations of the relationship and
distinctions between art and life, especially detachment and moral responsibility. The tone of *Loitering
with Intent* returns to that of the earlier novels, for it is
much more optimistic. Critical reactions were more
enthusiastic than those for several preceding novels.

The latest novel, *The Only Problem*, sustains the optimism of *Loitering with Intent* and contains Spark's
most rigorous religious discussion. Both are
reexaminations of ideas explored in Spark's first novel,
The Comforters. In *The Only Problem*, however, the
primary focus on the artist and autobiography is
replaced by a concentration on the most exacting
theological question: How can the person who believes
in God sustain a belief in a benevolent Creator when
confronted by the unspeakable sufferings of the world?
Through a thorough and learned exploration of
meanings of the Book of Job, and a delineation of a
modern man who lives a life analogous to the life of
Job, Spark shows a depth of understanding that transcends her earlier work. Set in contemporary France,
The Only Problem contains familiar details from the
popular press and detective stories—uncertain identity, erratic and exotic behavior, exploitation of
wealth, terrorism. The style retains its classic distinction; simplicity and clarity are combined with an
exquisite and often unexpected union of words. There
are also witty turns of phrase and hilarious parodies.
Even when exploring the most serious problem Spark
still manages to amuse. However, there is little self-
consciousness or indulgence. Spark achieves a finer
tone, a detachment and poise that are sustained by few
writers and come only as the achievement of the most
mature phase in a large body of work.

2

The Prime of Miss Jean Brodie

With *The Prime of Miss Jean Brodie*, Muriel Spark became famous and rich, a celebrated novelist with a wide audience. The title character of the novel fascinated readers and also became known through theater and cinema. Vanessa Redgrave first performed the role of the Scottish schoolteacher in Jay Presson Allen's play version in London in 1966, and Zoe Caldwell played Jean Brodie in New York. Maggie Smith won an Oscar for her creation of the role in the 1969 film, and Geraldine McEwan interpreted Miss Brodie for television audiences in the series shown on PBS in 1979. Jean Brodie and her "set" of girls became widely known, and a common response to the main character was, "I had a Jean Brodie in my life."

The novel has also elicited complex analyses from literary critics, many of whom judge it Spark's most distinctive and effective work. Such diversity of response—from popular media presentations with theatrical flair, to individual empathy, to arguments about theological and moral implications—is most appropriate to a writer noted for her wry wit, satirical view of human behavior, and examination of the nature of truth and art. Her audience's bafflement mirrors Spark's own view that, though everything is possible, no one individual can know reality. Thus personal assertions appear comically grotesque.

The Prime of Miss Jean Brodie is more a novella than a novel. Short, compact, and economical, it provides a useful introduction to Spark, who wrote it in eight weeks, calling on memories of her girlhood in Edinburgh. She has described the novel, which most explicitly uses her Scottish heritage, as the work of "an exile in heart and mind—cautious, affectionate, critical."[1] The play and film versions provided excellent vehicles for their stars; the charismatic schoolteacher compelled admiration, though Jean Brodie remained sufficiently ambiguous to complicate responses even with the simplification of dramatic presentation. Spark's fiction is more elusive and needs repeated careful and thoughtful readings to understand what lies below the surface appeal.

The main line of the narrative is not easy to discern, for there are many time shifts. Actually, these are crucial to the reader's understanding, for they force greater attention. The manipulation of time leads to something more than the amused delight that might be derived from a straightforward chronology that realistically tells the story of a dazzling eccentric and her impressionable students. Spark deliberately tells the reader early in the novel what the outcome of events will be, that Miss Brodie will be betrayed by her trusted pupil Sandy Stranger. With suspense eschewed, the interest lies in understanding why things happen rather than what happened.

This is further emphasized by the absence of explanations from Jean Brodie of why she behaves as she does. She is seen largely through the eyes of the girls, who speculate about their teacher. Although the novel includes events from a period of twenty years, the time when the "Brodie set" changed from pupils to adults, the concentration is on their girlhood experiences. And the major focus is on one girl, Sandy Stranger.

The Prime of Miss Jean Brodie begins in 1936, when the girls are sixteen and have moved out of the junior

division of the Marcia Blaine School for Girls in Edinburgh and Miss Brodie's class. Although they remain
"the Brodie set," proving the accuracy of their
teacher's maxim "Give me a girl at an impressionable
age, and she is mine for life," each now wears her hat
"with a definite difference." But the story soon shifts
back to those formative years, 1930 and 1931, when six
schoolgirls receive a remarkable education from a
"progressive spinster" who teaches in a school of
traditional character, serving as "a leaven in the
lump" at "this educational factory." Monica Douglas
("famous for mathematics and anger"), Jenny Gray
("who was going to be an actress"), Eunice Gardner
("famous for gymnastics and swimming"), Rose
Stanley ("famous for sex"), Mary Macgregor ("a silent
lump, a nobody whom everybody could blame"), and
Sandy Stranger ("merely notorious for her small,
almost nonexistent eyes" and "famous for her vowel
sounds"), are selected at age ten to be the *crème de la
crème*. Their formidable teacher epitomizes each as
"famous" for something and introduces all to her
romantic aesthetic vision. They adopt her taste for
Giotto, Pavlova, Sybil Thorndike, and the belief that
art comes before science. They have no "team spirit"
in the school and are a group set apart. Miss Brodie
declares that she is in her *prime*, which she defines as
"the moment one was born for," and she dedicates her
life to forming her girls, giving them "the fruits of her
prime."

The headmistress Miss Mackay, who believes in the
slogan "Safety First" and favors practical flowers like
chrysanthemums, schemes to rid the Marcia Blaine
School of Miss Brodie by discrediting her. However,
this is quite difficult, since all the girls in the set (except Mary Macgregor, who is a kind of scapegoat) are
clever and capable, and they admire their teacher.
Furthermore, Miss Brodie is vigilant and careful about
appearances, however outrageously she behaves.

The obvious possibility for discreditation is sex, particularly since in 1931, the year that the girls turn eleven and twelve and first become aware, "sex is everything." Both of the men teachers at the school are certainly interested in "a magnificent woman in her prime," and the girls increasingly recognize that "she was really an exciting woman as a woman." Teddy Lloyd, the art master, is the more dashing, for he lost an arm in World War I. But he is married and a Roman Catholic, and Jean Brodie finds a romantic renunciation of love far more exciting than an actual experience. She begins telling the girls of her lost lover Hugh, who died on Flanders Field, and gradually Teddy Lloyd's characteristics are fused into her fantasies. She also plans a surrogate affair using Rose, who is Lloyd's model (for pictures that all look like Jean Brodie). The other man is Gordon Lowther, the singing master, who is not married and an elder of the Church of Scotland. With him, Jean Brodie does have an affair, often staying at his home in Cramond. But she refuses to marry him, lest she be deterred from her dedication to her girls. Finally he marries the science teacher, Miss Lockhart, because he cannot tolerate Jean Brodie's distorted romanticism. Early in the novel, Sandy and Jenny presciently compare their teacher with their parents: she never got married, and they do not have primes, but they do have sexual intercourse.

The way to trap Miss Brodie is, then, politics, according to Sandy. This "beady eyed" girl, who is most like Miss Brodie in temperament and whose point of view dominates the story, becomes Teddy Lloyd's mistress in the summer of 1938, while Miss Brodie is touring in Germany to see what Hitler's brownshirts are like. In Nazi Germany the domineering Miss Brodie enlarges her earlier admiration for the Italian fascisti, the marching troops of blackshirts, seen in the previous summer's holidays, "with their hands raised at the same angle, while Mussolini stood on a platform like a gym teacher or Guides mistress and watched them." The comparison is a deliberate authorial comment, for Sandy Stranger views Miss Brodie as "a born Fascist." Sandy is not interested in politics, but she is obsessed with Miss Brodie. She tells Miss Mackay that Jean Brodie was responsible for sending Joyce Emily Hammond off to Spain, ironically not to join her brother's fight against Franco but to support the Fascist cause. This wretched girl, a latecomer and wouldbe member of the set, is killed in a train en route. Sandy gives the information to Miss Mackay, who then forces Miss Brodie to resign in 1939. Because Sandy recognizes that her teacher's manipulation of the set ignores their individuality and that she has no sense of the importance of another's life, Sandy decides that Jean Brodie's fascist control must be stopped.

By this time Sandy Stranger is no longer Teddy Lloyd's mistress, but she continues to admire his economical method of presentation and uses it in her betrayal of Miss Brodie. In less than a year, the man ceases to interest Sandy, though she was fascinated by his mind. The most important thing that she extracts from Lloyd's mind is his religion, and Sandy enters the Catholic Church. In this, she is in sharp contrast to Miss Brodie, who is contemptuous about Lloyd's religion. Sandy not only converts to the Church of Rome; she also enters an order of enclosed nuns.

As Sister Helena of the Transfiguration she writes "an odd psychological treatise on the nature of moral perception, called 'The Transfiguration of the Commonplace.' " In her middle age in the late 1950s, she is forced, because of this achievement, to have choice visitors even though her order is enclosed. She explains to an enquiring interviewer that the biggest influence on her was neither politics nor Calvinism, but "a Miss Jean Brodie in her prime." Some of her friends from schooldays also visit, and they talk of their teacher.

Always Sister Helena "clutches the bars of her grille," but "more desperately than ever" when she admits what most influenced her.

Miss Brodie spends her last years in the Braid Hills Hotel, trying to learn who "betrayed" her. She dies of cancer in 1946 when she is fifty-six years old. In one way, the novella is an account of this woman's rise and fall, but it also chronicles responses to her "prime." Muriel Spark has explained that she always begins with a title and then works out the story. Both as word and idea, "prime" resonates through the story. In no other work does she so relentlessly repeat a phrase, and the reader is led to a rich contemplation of the meanings of "prime of life" far beyond the narrative itself. The style of this short work, so evocative in its economy and simple language, reflected the experience of Spark's early poetic career. In an interview, Muriel Spark said that "Jean Brodie represents completely unrealized potentialities."[2] This broad statement of the theme provides a useful way of approaching the story's meaning.

The realistic details of *The Prime of Miss Jean Brodie* are unobtrusive, but so exactly introduced that they establish an immediate sense of time and place. The Edinburgh of the 1930s is vividly evoked in Chapter Two when Miss Brodie takes the girls on a walking excursion "into the reeking network of slums which the Old Town constituted in those years." This is a first direct experience for them away from the security of their middle-class homes. The poverty and desperation, the devastating loss of human possibility, are indicated in a single line: "A man sat on the icy-cold pavement, he just sat." They are stunned by the terrible smell of the area; they see men and women quarreling and a long queue of shabby men waiting for the Dole. Sandy is frightened by the squalor of the Unemployed, and she is aware of the discrepancy between these people and herself, though when she is

older she perceives a common misery that has nothing
to do with economics. Before World War II, she is
more concerned about relief in Edinburgh than events
on the Continent.

Spark is not a political novelist, but she is trying to
define the context in which she lived. *The Prime of
Miss Jean Brodie* corresponds to her own girlhood in
Edinburgh, and the historical significance is very important.[3] The Idle Unemployed are most obviously the
casualties of the economic depression that shattered
the Western world, as the last shudder of the Great
War and the wild extravagances of the 1920s that
followed it. The emerging Fascists are one answer to
the defeat and loss of spirit. Other casualties of World
War I are personally shown—the lost lover Hugh
Carruthers, the maimed art master, and Jean herself.

Only one of "the legions of her kind during the
nineteen-thirties, women from the age of thirty and
upward, who crowded their war-bereaved spin-
sterhood with voyages of discovery into new ideas and
energetic practices in art or social welfare, education,
or religion," Jean Brodie epitomizes the plight of the
Lost Generation, those who lived in a world where
traditional values and expectations had been
displaced. The romantic tales with which the teacher
regales her girls are an evasion of the realities of
human experience. The importance of fantasy in the
forming of the child is an accepted tenet of
sophisticated psychology, but the fantasy should result
in an increasingly mature understanding and coping
with human experience.

It is one thing for Sandy and Jenny to write romantic tales modeled on their favorite nineteenth-century
narratives, *Kidnapped*, *The Lady of Shalott*, and *Jane
Eyre*. This allows a relatively safe youthful exploration
of experience—and an opportunity for Muriel Spark to
write hilarious parodies of much-loved English classics
and sentimental love letters. But it is quite another

thing for forty-year-old Jean Brodie to substitute fantasies of lost and renounced lovers for recognition of her own sexuality, particularly when she wants the fantasy to turn into reality by having one of the girls take her place in Lloyd's bed. A reading of *The Prime of Miss Jean Brodie* as a menopausal crisis or unconscious lesbianism is far too simplistic, but the text provides enough evidence to suggest these possibilities. There is a fervid urgency about her creation of the "set" that argues a desperate lack of fulfillment, "the unrealized potentialities" that are salient.

Nevertheless, the novel can be described as a consideration of excessive self-indulgence, an exposition of the dangers and evil of a life that is concentrated solely in self. For, although Jean Brodie asserts that she is giving her prime to the schoolgirls, she is actually using them to avoid having to act herself, and her constant reiteration of her self-sacrifice limits the worth of whatever she does. Sandy early notes how Miss Brodie has "elected herself to grace." "She thinks she is Providence, thought Sandy, she thinks she is the God of Calvin, she sees the beginning and the end." Miss Brodie believes that God is on her side and has no idea of her own sinful nature. Hers is a very personal and secularized Calvinism.

The term "Calvinism" is used, of course, in many ways.[4] In *The Prime of Miss Jean Brodie*, Spark shows this view of humanity as a focal point of Edinburgh, and the characteristics that she emphasizes are a belief in the Elect and the Damned, the idea that man's salvation is predestined by God, and the idea of a community that is righteously and rigorously controlled. Nominally, Jean Brodie has rejected Edinburgh's Calvinism through her flamboyance, but in practice her *crème de la crème* are a secularized elect, the chosen elite selected from the larger group. Sandy deliberately contemplates the architectural landmarks of St. Giles Cathedral and the Tolbooth in an attempt to include the Calvinist theology that is lacking from her English experience. She also recognizes that Catholicism might have been what Miss Brodie lacked. But Sandy's own entry into the Roman Church is not a simplistic triumph of Catholic values. Her betrayal, her book, her spiritual condition—all lack certainty, as indeed is inevitable in this life, even for those who act decisively.

A manipulator of lives, Jean Brodie admires absolutist domination, as her attraction to Fascist leaders most clearly illustrates. Further, she is not capable of recognizing her own failures; even after World War II, she goes no farther than an admission that "Hitler *was* rather naughty." This grotesquely inadequate judgment is like her utter failure to recognize her culpability in treating Mary Macgregor with wanton unkindness, or in precipitating the death of the new girl Joyce Emily Hammond. And obviously she has not the slightest idea of how she influences Sandy Stranger, who betrays her precisely because she judges that no one should be allowed to exercise such unremitting control over the lives of others. (Paradoxically, of course, Sandy is behaving in the same controlling way; and her "small beady eyes" symbolize her limited, narrow vision.) Perhaps nothing so richly illustrates Jean Brodie's self-absorption as her incredulity that anyone could betray her—even Christ was betrayed, and He is God.

The novella, then, is concerned to define the nature of the human condition. The two principals, Jean Brodie and her near double Sandy Stranger (she actually assumes her teacher's role as Lloyd's mistress), know very little about it. Both fail to recognize its essentially mundane quality. The teacher refuses to admit the ordinary; she spins romantic fantasies to evade the limitations of life in this world—both those that come from political and social conditions and those that derive from personal blindness and pride.

The pupil becomes renowned for her psychological understanding of "The Transfiguration of the Commonplace." There is an undeniable appeal about escaping from the limits of mundane experience. This is the appeal of nineteenth-century romanticism, with its exaltation of the artist as one who is apart from society, a being more sensitive and suffering than others, who does not live by common standards. Muriel Spark repeatedly explored romanticism—and expressed antipathy to it.

Most members of the Brodie set—Eunice, Monica, Jenny, and Rose—grow beyond its narrow range into adults who are far less exotic and flamboyant than their mentor, but who live quietly and responsibly, able to resist impulses that would lead to the self-indulgences that destroy a perspective about human limitations. But Sandy, who is most like Jean Brodie, lacks such repose. In schoolgirl narratives, she casts herself as the heroine addressed by Alan Breck or Mr. Rochester or as the Lady of Shalott; she fantasizes about Pavlova's depending on her for the future of dance; she imagines herself as the right-hand woman of a mythical policewoman, in another fantasy that is a response to the ugly experience of Jenny's encounter with an exhibitionist. Even as a reclusive nun, she writes on the theme that has defined Jean Brodie's life and her own.

There are, of course, subtle differences. Sandy knows exactly what she is doing, while Jean Brodie is described as a kind of innocent. David Lodge has argued that the loss of primal innocence, the fallen world, is the subject of *The Prime of Miss Jean Brodie*, and that Sandy must betray Miss Brodie because she has so many bad qualities mixed with the good traits of enthusiasm, inspiration, and individuality.[5] But Sandy is not to be viewed without uneasiness; her hands "clutch the bars of her grille." She has withdrawn from the world; nevertheless, she has created a "set."

Sister Helena's book has more ardent admirers than
the selected schoolgirls at Marcia Blaine's School for
Girls. Her reclusive life may be viewed as a renunciation of the world to parallel her teacher's renunciation of a lover, or as a penance for the betrayal. But
even this does not work out according to plan, for she
lacks the repose of the other nuns in the community.
They notice her nervous tension and say that "Sister
Helena had too much to bear from the world since she
had published her psychological book which was so
unexpectedly famed." Nevertheless, the dispensation
that results in this exposure "was forced" upon her.
Once again, Spark shows how separated human expectations are from the realities of experience.

The "prime" of life is supposed to be a time of
realization, when the years of preparation and apprenticeship are turned into effective action, but the
novella shows how far Jean Brodie is from such
realization. The choice of the name "Brodie" is significant: Deacon William Brodie was an eighteenth-
century man whose reality was very different from appearances; he was the historical source for Robert
Louis Stevenson, another native of Edinburgh, whose
classic creation of the "double life," is *Dr. Jekyll and
Mr. Hyde.*[6] Publicly very respectable in civic and commercial enterprises, Deacon Brodie kept mistresses and
conducted night burglaries. He died cheerfully on the
gibbet, and his presence in Edinburgh remains very
visible today. At the corner of the Royal Mile and Bank
Street—in the Old Town that the Brodie set
visit—stands Deacon Brodie's Tavern, an imposing institution that was founded in 1806. This is precisely
the curious mixture of human experience that so
fascinated Muriel Spark. Thus the name "Sandy
Stranger" is also indicative, for it suggests both shifting
uncertainties and the fundamental apartness of all
people. Sandy is not simply the only English girl in the

set, the exile in Scotland, and the favorite who becomes a betrayer. She is also the essential human being who may act, but with unanticipated results.

The unexpected is what should be expected. The most trusted girl, the confidante, is the betrayer. But Sandy insists that "It's only possible to betray where loyalty is due." And loyalty was due to Miss Brodie "only up to a point," so that "the word [betrayal] does not apply." Just after Miss Brodie asserts that Lowther would marry her, she reads of his engagement. Mary Macgregor was not kindly treated, but she remembers her days in Miss Brodie's class as the happiest of her life. One must retain "a sense of the hidden possibilities in all things," for there are always startling revelations. This view of the world can be frightening, for it shows the limits of man's control, his woeful inadequacy and the absurdity of pretensions. Many in the modern world find this a despairing view, but Muriel Spark's faith prevents that conclusion.

Her vision is not limited to this world, for her fiction has both a literal and an allegorical level. The realistic narrative of life in Edinburgh in the 1930s is cogent, but it is only a small part of a much larger scheme. Spark amuses by writing a story about schooldays; she invigorates a strong literary tradition of boys' stories (like Thomas Hughes' *Tom Brown's Schooldays* [1857] and William Golding's *The Lord of the Flies* [1955]) by making her subjects girls—and very sophisticated ones, too. She updates the classic nineteenth-century feminist heroine Jane Eyre—a shy, earnest, plain governess living in an isolated house—into a dynamic twentieth-century woman —an exotic, good-looking, assured, witty teacher who moves freely about a large city and holidays alone on the Continent. The characteristics of the male lovers are exactly paralleled to underscore the analogy with Charlotte Brontë's novel, which the girls also rewrite in their own style. Nevertheless, the literary exactness, like the realistic account, is not the essential concern.

The shifting time sequence serves not only as an effective device to encompass events occurring over twenty years and to keep the reader alert to many possibilities. It also functions significantly to throw human actions into a larger perspective. The events in the girls' lives appear quite different from one time to another. As Miss Brodie's students, the girls are fascinated and absorbed by her fantasies and those that they create in imitation. As adults they perceive these events as relatively unimportant. So all events of this life, even its prime, are recognized as very small when placed in the context of a universe that is God's complex creation. The incidental details may not always be understood, but for the person of faith there is a belief in a design that is not contingent upon merely human actions. Thus the resort to self-indulgent power is a grotesque distortion, important and yet trivial and absurdly laughable.

Muriel Spark's comic vision, then, is not only a dazzling exploitation of witty language and outrageous circumstances in the present world. It is also an extended view of how inconsequential are human assumptions of knowledge and power when viewed in the light of eternity. This is a wisdom not shared by Jean Brodie and Sandy Stranger; the beady eyes do not see so far, but the novelist's view is much deeper, and it is her own point of view that Muriel Spark offers her readers.

3

Island Comforters

The Comforters

Muriel Spark's first novel, *The Comforters*, highly praised for its originality and wit, signaled the direction of her career. It was an appropriate inauguration to her novel writing because it was, among other things, an investigation of the writing of fiction. Spark described *The Comforters* as "a novel to work out the technique,"[1] and it revealed qualities that become much more refined in her later fiction. The author's constant interest in "voices" appears here both naturally and supernaturally. Her skillful mimicry of London talk, from middle-class Hampstead to intellectual Chelsea and somewhat sleazy Soho, evoked the society of the 1950s, with its continued sense of class difference. The heroine Caroline Rose also hears "voices." These make clear that, while she is having difficulty writing the chapter on realism in her critical study *Form in the Modern Novel*, she is also living in a novel that is being written and finally becomes *The Comforters*. More important than this aesthetic is Spark's introduction into *The Comforters* of theological questions, "realities" that are fundamental to her thought.

Caroline Rose is a highly intelligent and attractive young woman—"thin, angular, sharp, inquiring . . . well-dressed and good-looking." She is at a difficult stage in her life, for she is "grisly about the truth" and uncertain what truth is. As a consequence of her recent conversion to Roman Catholicism, she has ended the sexual part of her love affair with Lawrence Manders, a talented sports commentator for the BBC. However, she still very much wants and needs his company. At the beginning of *The Comforters*, Lawrence has gone to Sussex to stay with his grandmother, Louisa Jepp, while Caroline has gone on a religious retreat to The Pilgrim Centre of St. Philumena in Yorkshire. This establishment was recommended by Lawrence's mother Lady Helena who, having become a Catholic upon her marriage, is an energetic supporter of religious causes and unfortunate people. The father, Sir Edwin Manders, is a contemplative who spends more time on retreat than with his family. Their physical well-being rests on a fortune made through the Manders's Figs in Syrup business. The senior Manderses, then, are both much concerned with religion, one following the active and the other the contemplative way of life. Their son Lawrence has no faith and instead concerns himself only with facts.

Even as a boy, Lawrence noticed things. "He had terrorized the household with his sheer literal truths." Thus it is not surprising that he knows immediately that something strange is going on in Sussex. Lawrence has a talent for observation. He immediately recognizes that some of Louisa Jepp's acquaintances, her apparent financial resources, and free use of exotic items like Bulgarian cigarettes, argue the unusual. He has a detective's capacity for snooping and collecting details—like finding diamonds in a loaf of bread—but, as his half-gypsy grandmother notes, "the dear boy can't put two and two together." He knows that there is a mystery, and throughout the novel he is trying to discover exactly how his grandmother and her gang accomplish their smuggling.

Lawrence writes to Caroline because he knows that she has a capacity to get beyond his "merciless look of

reality." He has no religious faith, but his family
background makes him at least aware. Where Lawrence continues to examine things, "trying to detect
whatever it is he's looking for in life," Caroline has got
utterly beyond a world of physical reality. She finds
her old friend Eleanor Hogarth irritating because "she
has seemed not to change essentially in the years since
their Cambridge days together," and she is "indistinct,
in need of some touching up." An evening that
Caroline spends in Soho is a glimpse into the way she
was living with a sophisticated social group before she
"retreated from London." But the retreat is a disaster,
for Caroline finds that being a Catholic does not
eliminate difficulties. Indeed the people whom she
meets tend to be even less comforting than those she
has left behind. The horror of aggressive misap-
plication of religion is epitomized in Mrs. Georgina
Hogg, the resident manageress and a former nursery
governess in the Manders household. This "gargoyle"
so repulses Caroline that she flees to London and immediately tries to contact Lawrence, who is away at
his grandmother's cottage.

In an exhausted and highly nervous state, alone in
her flat, Caroline hears the sound of a typewriter, "immediately followed by a voice remarking her own
thoughts." Although she admits to being neurotic, she
is not willing to believe herself mad. There is,
however, at first no reasonable explanation, and
Caroline is frightened. She packs quickly and hurries
to the flat of an old friend, Willi Stock. Known to his
friends as "the Baron," this somewhat affected man is
a naturalized British subject who runs a bookshop in
Charing Cross Road. His less conventional activities
become clear as the novel develops; they are diabolism
and smuggling. The connections among all the characters are very close indeed, and part of the effectiveness
of *The Comforters* is Muriel Spark's suspenseful
narration of the interlocking plots that center on

mysterious voices and smuggling. Caroline and
Lawrence send telegrams to each other, and the
message is the same: "Come immediately something
mysterious going on."

Spark exploits the resources of detective fiction by
presenting clues and having her characters make some
connections, while still allowing the reader to work
out the mystery of Louisa Jepp's smuggling gang. A
seventy-eight-year-old grandmother is a somewhat
unlikely ringleader, and there is superb comic fun
made of the incongruity of this old lady's outsmarting
her clever grandson, her "London party/agents," and
the experienced criminals as well as the authorities.
She has a splendid capacity for reconciling disparate
elements, for avoiding the anxieties of others with a
sureness that neurotic Caroline can never master. The
two "mysteries" in *The Comforters*, then, are of a very
different order. A man like Lawrence can only garner
facts; he does not really comprehend either his grandmother's "coordinating the inconsistent elements of experience" or Caroline Rose's experience of the voices.
He tries to capture the voices on a tape recorder, while
Caroline observes, "This sound might have another
sort of existence and still be real."

Caroline's condition is a result of her dissatisfaction
with the merely comfortable and amusing life that she
has lived in London as a writer and Lawrence's
mistress. She perceives her own limitations and those
of her social group: they are neither loyal nor
genuinely concerned about anything except themselves, for "each one discourses upon his private obsession regardless." The Baron, who is a nexus of this
Bohemian world and Louisa's partner in smuggling,
answers affirmatively when Caroline asks: "Is the
world a lunatic asylum then? Are we all courteous
maniacs discreetly making allowances for everyone
else's derangement?" Even the Baron, however, shows
a need for something more than civil posturing; he is

fascinated with Satanism and desperately urges that Mervyn Hogarth, who is later revealed as Eleanor Hogarth's husband, is the most important diabolist in England. Thus the Baron can at least talk with Caroline, who is described as "mystic." His obsession with Black Masses parallels her membership in the Church. Spark is not simply showing two polarized alternatives; she is also making clear how difficult it is to know the truth, what is real.

One of Caroline's difficulties is balancing the claims of individuality that characterize her former life with the claims of community that the Church enjoins. When she finds herself at the retreat house she knows all too clearly how hard it is to follow the precepts of Christianity:

> The demands of the Christian religion are exorbitant, they are outrageous. Christians who don't realise that from the start are not faithful. They are dishonest: their teachers are talking in their sleep. "Love one another . . . brethren, beloved . . . your brother, neighbors, love, love, love"—do they know what they are saying?

The particular occasion for Caroline's difficulty is Georgina Hogg, whose "colossal bosom" sickens the prim and fastidious Caroline.

As her name "Hogg" indicates, this woman is massively large and overpowering in her relentless assertion of Catholic community. She intrudes upon Caroline and everyone else. Her entire life has been characterized by dominating others, most grotesquely perhaps in her failed marriage to Mervyn Hogarth (Hogg) and in intermittent appearances to receive assistance from Helena Manders, so that the family calls her "Manders's Mortification." Eleanor Hogarth rhetorically calls her a "witch," and the Baron believes that she is literally a witch. Caroline recalls her as "Not a real-life character, only a gargoyle." Spark repeats this term to introduce the damaging description "as soon as Mrs. Hogg stepped into her room she disappeared, she simply disappeared. She had no private life whatsoever. God knows where she went in her privacy." On the drive to the fatal picnic when Georgina Hogg is drowned, both the Baron and Helena see her disappear from the back seat; and Caroline suggests, "Maybe she has no private life whatsoever." Helena explains more fully that because Mrs. Hogg has nothing in her life she has been nosey. In fact, she has always been a threatening moral blackmailer.

Georgina Hogg is, then, a kind of allegorical figure. She vividly represents the unappealing individuals who are part of the community of the Church—the reality of persons as well as the intellectual ideas. Indeed as Edwin Manders observes, "Caroline was an odd sort of Catholic, very little heart for it, all mind," so that her confrontation with Georgina is a severe test. Helena has repeatedly put the wretched woman in new situations as part of her charitable work. An active doer of good, she too evades certain realities, for "she was happiest when life could be reduced to metaphor, but life on its lofty literal peaks oppressed her." Helena recognizes, however, her limits, her difficulty in accepting something like the relationship of Lawrence and Caroline or having a lucid idea of her husband's homosexual brother Ernest.

The problem is basic—how to achieve a balance between charity and perception. The test for Caroline comes when, at the picnic, Helena asks her to "be an angel," to take the small boat across the river and bring Georgina back to avoid the rain. Spark describes the situation carefully: Caroline is being asked for "more than an ordinary favor"; she takes "a plunge against nature"; and Helena describes the act as "really charitable." Caroline suppresses her physical repulsion to give Georgina a helping hand. When the huge woman slips and tips over the boat, she clutches

Caroline's hand fiercely and pulls her down into the water; in panic she grasps the smaller woman's throat. Only because Caroline knows how to hold her breath and does not struggle, does she escape when Georgina's grip slackens as she drowns. In this episode Caroline is "involved personally," her requirement for a religious life. In spite of Georgina's repulsiveness, Caroline suspends judgment and serves one who is in need. Further, she lives on to finish the novel that she is writing. This is possible partially because of her effort, but there is also something outside Caroline that contributes. The novel mysteriously incorporates a letter that Lawrence had torn up before sending it to her. The resolution of Caroline's problems indicates that she is following Edwin Manders's advice that the novel should be "an old fashioned one, ending with the death of the villain and the marriage of the heroine." With many conflicts resolved and nervousness alleviated, Caroline playfully jokes about going to finish her work; it is a "holiday of obligation." This pun on the Catholic practice of "holy days of obligation" (obligatory attendance at Mass), suggests a pleased acceptance of her role, a letting go of self.

A rather cheerful note is characteristic of *The Comforters*. The title alludes to the Book of Job, a scriptural text of special interest to Spark while she was writing the novel. She noted how the comforters fail to understand each other or Job, so that both the suffering and the comforting are to be survived.[2] Nevertheless, Spark clearly is satirical when she describes Caroline's previous society as one in which "It was understood that every close association between two people was a perversion."

The presentation of Edwin's "retreat" into contemplation suggests that this way of life is not adequate. He cannot cope with his daily affairs, the inevitable emergencies. Edwin, like Caroline, is described as a "mystic," and his "ascent by the winding stair" suggests the English fourteenth-century mystic Walter Hilton. But Edwin's remoteness from the world, his living almost entirely "a life of interior philosophy," is unsatisfactory. At the end of the novel, he admits that his retreats have been too frequent; he recognizes how he has succumbed to spiritual temptations. Finally accepting that he would not have succeeded as a religious, he returns to a more active life and pays attention to family affairs.

Caroline risks a similar withdrawal, being caught up in the intellectual life of the Church, while evading much of its more taxing demand to "love neighbors." The tension produces her nervous anxiety, but, through the voices that she has time to listen to while she recovers from the injuries received in a car crash, she gains insight. She achieves the perilous balance between caring and not caring, the mystic condition of stasis. In *The Comforters*, this poise is also described as managing a coherent narrative, when she is "at last outside it, and at the same time consummately inside it." She is concerned about her personal relations, but she is not obsessed by them. She does not ignore the realistic details of everyday existence, but she knows that there is another kind of reality. At the start of the novel, Caroline questions Georgina Hogg, who says that "Our Lady has spoken to me," about whether the voice was actual/audible. The reply is that words come only to one who is experienced in the spiritual life. Soon afterward Caroline hears her voices, amusingly modernized to sound with the tap-tapping of a typewriter.

Whoever hears voices, as Caroline recognizes, is believed "a little cracked in the head . . . slightly insane . . . out of my senses . . . neurotic." In *The Comforters*, Muriel Spark indicated that she was concerned with something more than the natural world, that indeed the events of the so-called "real" world are comparatively absurd or at least unpredictable. But she had not yet developed the technical mastery for fully integrating diverse elements, so there was more exposition than realization. Similarly, the brilliant compression of her later poetic style was here only suggested by the precise handling of dialogue. The novelist was examining her form while practicing it, and *The Comforters* showed exciting promise that would be developed into controlled perfection in Spark's later fiction.

Robinson

There are several resemblances between Muriel Spark's first two novels; however, *Robinson* is more systematically ordered and obvious than *The Comforters* in its treatment of themes and characters. The narrative details are quite exact. On the way to the Azores, a small plane carrying twenty-nine passengers crashes on Robinson, a tiny island, on 10 May 1954. There are only three survivors, all rescued by the island's reclusive owner. A man of fifty-one, Robinson has withdrawn to solitary existence because of his sense of the world's inadequacy.

The story is told in the first person by January Marlowe, a widow whose teenaged son Brian is in school in England. She is a journalist—"poet, critic, and general articulator of ideas"—and keeps a journal of her time on the island, portions of which are introduced into the narrative. The other two survivors are men, and January notes "their joint intelligence was probably not superior to mine." Jimmie Waterford is a relative of Robinson and was coming to ask him to return to Gibraltar to look after Robinson's extensive inheritance, or at least to secure the authority to do this himself. Tom Wells is less appealing and sophisticated. A blackmailer, he sells charms that are reputed to bring luck and publishes a magazine called *Your Future* to foster his occult interests. The only other inhabitant of the island is a nine-year-old boy, Miguel, an orphan whom Robinson has befriended and who will soon be going away to school.

There is no means of communication from the island, so the survivors must wait until August, when the pomegranate boat regularly comes to deliver stores and bring workers to harvest Robinson's crop. Thus the novel has a tightly circumscribed quality. Almost classical unities are observed: the setting is limited to the island, the time to three months, and the action to Robinson's disappearance. What happens "was only to be expected. . . . Human nature does not vary much." Each of the three survivors rushes to assume the authority left in abeyance when Robinson disappears, and all suspect each other of his apparent murder. Just before the boat arrives, Robinson reappears, and the survivors go back home, while Miguel will soon leave for school. Once again, Robinson will be alone on his island.

Any narrative that is set on an island and has the title *Robinson* clearly belongs to the long tradition of adventure stories that begins with Daniel Defoe's *Robinson Crusoe*, is brilliantly developed in satirical form in Jonathan Swift's *Gulliver's Travels*, continues with imitations like *The Swiss Family Robinson*, and persists in the Robinson family of the popular American television series *Lost in Space* and the more exacting novel of William Golding, *The Lord of the Flies*. Countless tales of castaway survival are simply adventure stories, but often they raise serious moral questions. Muriel Spark's *Robinson* is so strongly religious and psychological that these are the overtones, while the island adventure and the murder mystery are the undertones.

As in a classic detective story, there are an apparent murder and a limited number of suspects. The first-person narrator serves as chief investigator, searching for the body, controlling the available arms, considering "who done it," and even giving two full journal entries that summarize her findings and arguments of possible guilt as though she were a master detective summing up the case. This provides excitement and challenge. The careful descriptions of the island, of which Spark even provides a map, give an interesting sense of place. But such detail is not of primary interest.

The opening sentence of *Robinson* encourages speculative reading; January Marlowe says that her stay on the island "was a time and landscape of the mind." The last paragraph of the book repeats her view of "the island as a place of the mind . . . an apocryphal island." This point of view is the crucial aspect of her journey, not the tangible realities like her journal, the newspaper clippings about the crash and return, or the cat Bluebell that Robinson gave her when she left. As in *The Comforters*, Spark is investigating the nature of reality, truth, religious belief, personal isolation, and the importance of community. Her basic serious asking of questions is again overlaid with narrative skills and verbal dexterity. Admiring Jimmie, January admits that she is "a pushover for a story" and, like most readers, "will more or less always take kindly to the raconteur type." In *Robinson* Spark sought a similar sympathetic response; her style is personal and engaging. The novel is, however, more explicit than her earlier fiction, so that the narrative almost seems to exist as a frame for exploring ideas.

There are many clues that *Robinson* can be read allegorically. The island's topography resembles the body of a man, and Robinson has named the parts appropriately—The Headlands, The North and South Arms, The West Leg, and so on, as well as Tunnels and a Furnace in the interior. Because he is not a man at ease with himself, he cultivates the Headland and ignores the rest. The proper names of the characters are also symbolic: January for Janus, the god who looks both ways, and Marlowe, the character in Joseph Conrad who asks questions. Tom Wells combines the ordinary with a hint of hidden energy in irrational depths. Jimmie (a burglar's crowbar) Waterford (an easy place to cross a river) suggests a compromise. Marlowe, Wells and Waterford are all English place names, just as Robinson is the name of both the owner and the island. Robinson's given names "Miles Mary" suggest both militant authority ("miles" is Latin for soldier) and the Virgin Mary; and Robinson is a violent opponent of Marianism in the Catholic Church. He regards this "superstitious idolatry," and the rosary which is used for prayer to Mary, as evil. Indeed Robinson's book *The Dangers of Marian Doctrine*, written before he stopped training for the priesthood and withdrew from the world, denounced this popular part of Catholicism as heresy.

While Robinson gives his name to the novel, the story is very much that of January. Thus allegorical interpretations can be a simple contrast between youth, romance, illusion and age, experience, truth. January's perceptions during her stay on the island are quite different from those she has when she is back in Chelsea thinking about what has happened. One critic[3] has advanced an elaborate reading in which January's isolation on the island is a psychic experience in which her personality splits in the characteristic Freudian way. Robinson in this scheme represents the superego, Jimmie the ego, and Wells the id. There is, then, a kind of climax when Wells meets and attacks January in the tunnels. She escapes and finds that Robinson has returned: ordered control is restored.

There is also much material in the novel to support a reading of distinctions between male and female minds, stereotypically viewed as rational and intuitive. Robinson repeatedly tells January to "Stick to facts" and abjures feelings, yet he recounts legends about the island and stages the "bloody" murder.

January notes that "the pagan mind runs strong in women at any time," but she asserts that she is a Christian and thus resists the temptation "to throw wider her arms and worship the moon." She treasures the rosary and fosters prayer to Mary, while he tries to remove this dangerous Earth mythology. To January, the lost Robinson becomes "the heroic character of a pagan pre-Christian victim of expiation." She may be annoyed by his aloofness, but she recognizes his kindness and that he has saved the lives of the three intruders into his island sanctuary. Like the Good Samaritan, he provides, but he goes on his own way.

There is thus a paradoxical situation: Robinson persists in giving the lie to the classic statement "No man is an island," but he is consistently generous in dealing with others' physical needs. He cares for the orphaned Miguel, nurses the three survivors, tries terribly hard to amuse them, and gives his stores generously. He even halves his supply of cigarettes with January, and never protests when she takes more than her share as a way of expressing her distress about his detached manner. Further, he shows no anger when the secrets of his island, his adoptive son (January teaches Miguel to say the rosary in spite of Robinson's plea that she not), and even his cat are taken over. What Robinson fears is "any material manifestation of grace." Even if his guests were not singularly ungenerous and self-centered—like the humans he has left the world to avoid—he would still have no faith in goodness. His life is one of withdrawal, he expects that people will behave badly, and he cannot imagine love. January's final evaluation of him as "a selfish but well-meaning eccentric" seems accurate.

January is potentially a Robinson figure. She has intelligence, competence, and determination. In her early and brief marriage, motherhood, widowhood, and recent conversion to Catholicism, she has been very self-sufficient. She is gathering material for a book about islands at the time of the crash. January makes clear in her first-person narrative, however, that, although she fears over-familiarity, she also recognizes her humanity. Limitations and failures mingle with strengths. She admits, "My moods are not stable at the best of times," and "The truth is, I have a sharp tongue when I am annoyed." She describes her deliberate little acts of meanness—spilling soup on Tom Wells, putting sugar in his tea, taking extra cigarettes "to mortify her immortal soul," and provoking Robinson about music and cabaret, dressing in gypsy disguise to get at her puritanical brother-in-law Ian Brodie. She also admits her vanity about make-up. She admits she is so inquisitive about people that she becomes a snoop in their private possessions, as had Lawrence Manders in *The Comforters*. Her fascination with faces leads her to imitative con- tortions in the hope of understanding. She does not judge solely by appearances, but she is fascinated, "I seek no justification for this habit, it is one of the things I do."

This is not smug complacency but a larger ac- ceptance that characterizes January's thought. She resents Robinson's failure to cultivate the island, to plant and nourish rather than live on tinned goods. She objects to Ian Brodie, who is several times described as impotent and a prurient puritan. Where Robinson asserts that his actions are "beyond the ob- vious range," January insists "there's no such thing as a private morality." Here she echoes exactly Caroline Rose's judgment that "you have to be personally in- volved." Thus her other brother-in-law Curly Lons- dale is the preferred relative, because, for all his com- monness, he has a generosity, kindliness, and vitality that delight her son Brian and that January ex- periences upon her return. Curly insists that her sur- vival is "an occasion" and that all must be cheerful. He gets rid of the reporters and brings her breakfast in bed while she recovers and adjusts.

Most importantly January believes that one can live only in a system that "allows for the unexpected and unwelcome." She does not write the book on the three islands, but she is a survivor. From her experience of Robinson she gains perspective. She returns to live in a community, however difficult its members (though no one is a grotesque like Georgina Hogg), and yet maintains a detachment. She knows that the unexpected occurs at every moment. The events described in the journal are "transformed"; no words ever completely encompass because life is beyond description. The island itself, she reads in the newspaper, is sinking into the sea.

Early in the narrative January rejects the idea that it would have been better if she had not taken the journey that ended in a crash, just as she "rejects the idea that it is best to have never been born." And her last words reaffirm that "immediately all things are possible." The final lines of a Muriel Spark novel, like the concluding couplet of a Shakespearean sonnet, often provide a basic statement. Here January's conclusion is an assertion of faith, and the idea is one that is reiterated in later works.

January Marlowe is a more poised heroine than Caroline Rose. Spark's playful wit appears on almost every page, and there are amusing incidents like teaching a cat to play ping pong. Jimmy's strange way of speaking English provides constant humor. He learned the language "first from a Swiss uncle, using Shakespeare and some seventeenth-century poets as textbooks, and Fowler's *Modern English Usage* as a guide, and secondly from contact with Allied forces during the war." January's observations are often wittily devastating, and she enjoys jokes. When she reads in Tom Wells' account of their adventure that "Jan was a brick," she remarks, "Would that I were, I thought, and I would hurl myself at his fat head." Thinking about the habit of English Catholics to follow a meal with the prayer for the faithful departed "suggests to my mind that we have eaten them." January even sees a comic side to Robinson's elaborate staging of his disappearance.

Spark's humor is here more outrageously funny than terrifying. When Jimmie fires the pistol at Wells' head, "Nothing happened, not even a click." There are personal jokes; the title itself is a pun, since Robin is Spark's son's name. She includes other private jokes like "MURIEL THE MARVEL with her X-ray eyes. *Can read your very soul.* Scores of satisfied clients . . ." as one of the advertisements in *Your Future.* There is a zesty exuberance and confidence that suggest the masterworks she produced in the next years, when phrases like "in your prime" and suggestions that "You've got to die sometime" were fully explored.

4

Memento Mori

Regarded by many critics as Muriel Spark's masterpiece, *Memento Mori* was indeed a great achievement.
The novel is her most relentlessly restrictive and at the
same time her most expansive. While its subject and
characters are limited, its theme is universal, for the
one certainty in life is that death comes to all. *Memento Mori* is concerned with aging and death, and the
characters are almost all in their seventies or eighties.
Spark precisely observes the elderly in their in-
capacities and in their frequent selfish pettiness and indulgences, but the novel is no bleak catalogue of infirmity and decline. Its short, concentrated narrative
includes an undiminished respect for human poten-
tiality and perseverance. A geriatric community seems
an unlikely place to generate comedy or mystery and
suspense, yet these are the artistic techniques used to
great effect by Spark who uses many of the manners of
the detective story. She seriously considers basic questions about the mystery of existence, but the novel is
deft and witty.

The action, set in London in the 1950s, is rather
simple. A group of people, most of whom have known
each other for a lifetime, have shared many experiences, and now each has the same experience but
individually. The telephone rings, the person answering identifies him or herself, and the voice of the

caller says, *"Remember you must die."* Only these words are spoken. The message is always the same, but not the caller. Sometimes the voice is that of a young man, another time it is middle-aged, old, or even boyish; and one time it is a woman's voice.

The novel begins with a telephone call to Dame Lettie Colston. She is seventy-nine years old and at the time had received eight previous calls of the same nature. By the end of the novel, two years later, Dame Lettie has been gruesomely murdered by an unidentified burglar in her house in Hampstead, an elegant London district. Her telephone caller is a middle-aged man whose voice, like the woman herself, is strong and sinister. A lifelong volunteer worker in prisons, at heart Dame Lettie is an envious and vicious woman. She tries, for example, to control her nephew Eric by taunts about her will; and she denigrates his mother Charmian, who was a very attractive woman and a successful novelist but is now frail and sometimes confused at the age of eighty-five. Charmian is the wife of Lettie's brother Godfrey. When Lettie tells him about the telephone calls that have been going on for six weeks, Godfrey dismisses the caller, saying, "He must be a maniac."

As the novel develops, each of the old friends receives a call, reminding them that they must die; but attempts to identify the caller remain unsuccessful. Alec Warner, who is such a "pure realist" that he expresses doubts about whether people exist, spends his time doing research on old age, recording on file cards the reactions of all his old friends. At first he thinks the calls are only imagined; but when he receives one himself, he asks whether there is general hysteria. Percy Mannering, who is a poet, turns the message into a line for a Shakespearean sonnet called "Memento Mori." Guy Leet, a critic with whom Mannering has many literary quarrels, does not "mind a bit of fun." Though badly crippled, Guy retains much of the lively charm that attracted Charmian fifty years earlier when they were first lovers. Mabel Pettigrew also receives a call. She is a snoop and a blackmailer who uses her position as Charmian's companion to acquire damaging evidence that threatens Godfrey's precious pretence before his wife. Interested in power and getting money from old victims, the evil Mrs. Pettigrew denies having gotten a message and smugly continues in her grasping ways. To her, the call Godfrey received was just imagined. Godfrey, a robust eighty-seven, "wonderful for his age," drinks a whiskey and thinks of his present feelings. His erotic desires are now satisfied by looking at a woman's naked thigh, an old man's lust persisting after the many affairs of his youth. He is always gauging whether his old acquaintances have "lost their faculties," and he feels most fit and cheerful whenever Charmian is less clear mentally. Having been aware for years of his inferiority to his charming, successful wife, Godfrey now enjoys dominating her. But he remains anxious lest she recognize his deficiencies.

Since all the characters know each other, there is constant interaction among them. There are large group scenes like those at Lisa Brooke's funeral and at the house of Henry Mortimer, a retired detective who is asked to investigate the calls. Several of the characters (Dame Lettie, Alec Warner, Guy Leet) also go to the Maud Long Medical Ward to visit Jean Taylor, Charmian's longtime companion until her retirement. Taylor entered this geriatric establishment when her arthritis became so incapacitating that she could no longer live alone. Jean Taylor, who is eighty-two, receives no telephone calls. However, as she explains to her former lover, Alec Warner, the senile group in the "granny" ward are "our memento mori. Like your telephone calls."

The old women in the state hospital are all too poor to be in elegant private nursing homes like the one to which Charmian goes in the course of the novel. They provide a sharp contrast to the wealthy, sophisticated, and privileged members of Charmian's group. Economic differences, however, serve largely to emphasize a likeness of circumstance. Everyone grows old and receives the message *"Remember you must die,"* either as a private telephone call or by seeing others who are nearer to death. Among the old there are differences, as becomes vividly clear when the senile cases are put into the ward. Or when Granny Bean, who as a girl once saw Queen Victoria, celebrates her one hundreth birthday, there is a cause for reflection.

Making one see the limits of earthly life is a prime objective of *Memento Mori.* But as the old people live out their last years, they recall their youth. Charmian, for example, remembers the fuss about Garibaldi during her childhood. Her novels which "once set the literary world on fire" were written before World War I and also pleased a new audience when they were reissued after World War II. Charmian's love affairs with Guy Leet occurred from 1902 to 1907 and then again in 1926. She is finally confronted by Godfrey, whom Jean Taylor has told of his wife's infidelity so that he can be free of Mrs. Pettigrew's blackmail. Vanity no longer seems important, for "Charmian began to laugh, and could not stop, and eventually had to be put to bed." Infidelity and concealment, mutual delusions, seem absurd to a woman who has put them behind her as she thinks of her own death.

Guy Leet and Percy Mannering quarrel violently about a critical judgment of a poet; they actually exchange physical blows, each using one of Guy's two walking sticks. After Leet asks him to stay overnight, Mannering remains three weeks. Spark thus raises questions about the magnitude and reality of all actions. The novel concludes with a scene between Alec Warner and Jean Taylor. The realist lost all his scientific notes for his nine-year study of Old Age in a fire four months earlier, and since then he has felt "really dead." Jean Taylor observes, "We all appear to ourselves frustrated in our old age, Alec, because we cling to everything so much." The image of man's worldly efforts going up in smoke is a powerful conclusion, a reiteration of the primary theme of the novel: the limitations of worldly achievement.

Only a few characters among those whom Spark created, have an understanding of this; they are Jean Taylor and Charmian, both Roman Catholics whose traditional religious values rest upon a belief in life after death, and also Henry Mortimer, who asserts that a remembrance of death "intensifies" life, which is "insipid" without it. He does not "attempt to express a specifically religious point of view," and he has not described himself as a "mystic." There is, however, a similarity between his understanding and that of Jean and Charmian, because his view of life includes more than himself. The other significant resemblance that Mortimer and his wife share with Taylor and Charmian is a quiet and repose that all the others lack, as well as a concern for others and a detachment from self.

Godfrey finds the experience of receiving a call from Lettie's caller "unpleasant"; but Charmian advises against extreme reaction, "Well, I should treat it as it deserves to be treated. . . . Neither more nor less." When the voice asks for her and says *"Remember you must die,"* Charmian cheerfully replies, "Oh, as to that, for the past thirty years and more I have thought of it from time to time. My memory is failing in certain respects. I am gone eighty-six. But somehow I do not forget my death, whenever that will be." However, when she says good-bye, she asks, "What paper do you represent?" Thus she identifies the voice as a reporter, one of the many who continue their interest in Charmian Piper, the novelist. She may not know the identity of the caller or she may be behaving in her characteristic evasive way. Much of Charmian's attractiveness lies in her kindly innocence, but she is so determined to be agreeable that she evades difficult truths. Throughout the years, she has never confronted Godfrey. She has lived "reasonably" with him by never touching his pride directly and by remaining silent about his infidelities. Now, though she knows that Godfrey is dominating her and she is frightened, she lacks the courage to break the pattern of avoiding the truth, the game of fifty years, for which Godfrey would not forgive her, since the "simple idea of *facing* each other . . . is terrible." She rationalizes that "too much candour in married life is an indelicate modern idea."

Charmian, then, leads her life as she once wrote novels. Indeed in her old age it is her novels and the past, not the present, about which she has no confusion. The results are agreeable, and the surface is polished brilliantly, but there are disturbing limits. Her perseverance, for example, in the touching scenes when she prepares her tea without assistance, is powerful, yet the dominant impression is of a life that lacks repose. Talking to Guy Leet about her novels, Charmian explains that she always got into a tangle, "Because," she says, "the art of fiction is very like the practice of deception." This statement, one that is frequently quoted in discussions of Muriel Spark, echoes ideas from *The Comforters*. The novelist is uneasy about her art, the way in which the creation both reveals and obscures truth. Guy Leet continues, "And in life is the practice of deception in life an art too?" Whatever her practice may have been, Charmian's reply indicates that she makes the crucial distinction: "In life," she said, "everything is different. Everything is in the Providence of God. When I think of my own life . . . Godfrey . . . "

Charmian's Roman Catholicism has taught her that there are two kinds of reality, a world that is Caesar's and another that is God's. Her mind is not always

clear, but she makes a firm decision and leaves Godfrey to go to the nursing home. The reason that she
gives for the change is to get away from the telephone
calls; and once away from the familiar circle, Charmian becomes more alert and feels an "innocence . . .
almost free from Original Sin." Then she worries
about Godfrey and finally stops hiding the truth from
him. Perhaps Charmian's laughter means that, at last,
she has achieved the detachment that has long eluded
her, so that she knows the absurdity of her life.

When Charmian converted to Roman Catholicism,
her companion Jean Taylor entered the Church to
please her. However, in fact, it is not the novelist's but
her follower's life that becomes meaningfully
religious. In the summer of 1907 Alec Warner and
Jean Taylor were lovers, but the affair was broken off.
As late as 1928 she thought him strange; clearly his
view that facts are everything is not compatible with
her religious outlook. They frequently talk about
reality. Alec represents the scientific approach:
modern man records all of the observable details, and
his intellect makes it possible for him to analyze the
physical world. Alec has no trepidation about using his
friends and reducing them to notes and cards in his
file. Some of the most outrageous humor in the novel
comes from this research sociologist's habit of pressing
his friends to record their temperatures and pulses
before and after any unusual experience.

In the last years of her life Jean is impatient with her
former lover's reductions, and "for a moment utterly
hated him" when they disagreed about death. "A good
death," she said, "doesn't reside in the dignity of
bearing but in the disposition of the soul." He hates
her and demands, "Prove it," to which she replies,
"Disprove it." This violent opposition is an epitome of
the two views of existence and the unlikelihood of
altering convictions. Jean Taylor, the individual in
whom others most confide, does not try to change

others, but she holds to her belief. While Charmian declares that in life Providence controls, Jean actually lives this belief.

Jean Taylor is the first to identify the maker of the telephone calls. Significantly, this occurs during a Mass and is identified by Spark as "an irrational idea." Taylor and another granny arranged the Mass for the soul of Granny Barnacle, a noisy, troublesome patient and a former prison inmate "who had no relatives to mourn her." Jean has silently endured unusual pain throughout the night and refused to ask for an injection, lest the nurses prevent her from participating in the Mass. "This irrational idea" comes, then, with self-discipline, restraint, and self-abnegation. She "dismissed it and concentrated on her prayers," but it comes to her repeatedly.

To know, however, is not to influence others. Thus, when Dame Lettie goes on and on about her fears and suspicions, "Miss Taylor felt reckless."

"In my belief," she said, "the author of the anonymous telephone calls is Death himself, as you might say. I don't see, Dame Lettie, what you can do about it. If you don't remember Death, Death reminds you to do so. And if you can't cope with the facts the next best thing is to go away for a holiday."

Dame Lettie, of course, thinks that Jean has "taken leave of her senses" and tells the nurse that she is "off her head and should be watched." Any recognition of the supernatural, then, results in one's being judged mad, and the secularized modern world regards such ideas as menacing.

The other character in *Memento Mori* who knows the identity of the telephone caller is Henry Mortimer, but he shares the knowledge only with his wife. Her trust and admiration of her husband are unperceived by others, but Mortimer knows his wife to be utterly understanding, even though his children and grandchildren do not take him seriously. He also concludes and tells his wife, "considering the evidence, in my opinion the offender is Death himself." With the others, he is much more cautious. He talks quietly with those who have had calls, gives them a good tea, and then explains:

If I had my life over again I should form the habit of nightly composing myself to thoughts of death. I would practice, as it were, the remembrance of death. There is no other practice which so intensifies life. Death, when it approaches, ought not to take one by surprise. It should be part of the full expectancy of life. Without an ever-present sense of death life is insipid. You might as well live on the whites of eggs.

Mortimer asserts as a truth that "to remember one's death is a way of life," but, remaining a policeman, he talks of motives and evidence, making "little sermons that help to pass the time." He does not identify the "man," even when asked directly. His nightly remembrance of death is very close to the Catholic nightly prayer for a happy death, but Mortimer later denies that he is making a religious statement. His point is not a belief in the supernatural, but simply an acceptance of death as part of the basic cycle of all lives. Mortimer's life embodies this principle. Only he is presented as a family man; there are references to his grandchildren and a warm scene in which he plays with one of them. His other main interest is gardening, another symbol of a life-death cycle.

Jean Taylor and Henry Mortimer share the role of counselor to others and are similar in their calm repose. But Mortimer is not on Taylor's level. He is a good man but one who is, nevertheless, still defining himself only in the natural world. She is much more rigorous in her thought and action; she no longer maintains social pretences. Jean Taylor is closer to God than to humans. Her situation may be described

as that of a contemplative rather than an active person. Confined to her bed, she suffers considerable
pain, but she has transcended these trivialities. She has
reached a stage in which her being is all directed to
God:

> After the first year she resolved to make her suffering a
> voluntary affair. If this is God's will then it is mine. She
> gained from this state of mind a decided and visible dignity,
> at the same time as she lost her stoical resistance to pain.

Even the usually insensitive hospital staff recognize
the difference between her and the other "grannies."
Whatever suffering and humiliation Jean Taylor
knows, they are insignificant because she experiences
everything as "the Will of God." Unlike the others,
Taylor does not fuss about a will, or fear the winter, or
feel anxious that the nursing staff will neglect or
mistreat her. She has reached a point of spiritual ease
and has no fear of old age or dying. Appropriately
Memento Mori ends with a statement about the individual who has most detached herself from worldly
duress: "Jean Taylor lingered for a time, employing
her pain to magnify the Lord, and meditating
sometimes confidingly upon Death, the first of the
Four Last Things to be ever remembered."

The phrasing of the last line is crucial, for it iterates
that Death is not the end but the beginning. Death is
only the *first* of the four last things; the others,
Judgment, Heaven, and Hell, will follow. This is basic
to Christian belief and an understanding of *Memento
Mori*. The unflinching delineation of old age and personal failings is not simply macabrely witty satire.
Spark has focused on old people because they ought to
be most aware of and responsive to the message,
"Remember you must die." However, she is much less
concerned with young and old than she is with the
relation of temporal and eternal. With this perspective, it is clear that all the concern about im-

mediate events is insignificant. Alec Warner questions Jean Taylor when she decides to reveal Charmian's love affair to Godfrey, and she replies, "There is a time for loyalty and a time when loyalty comes to an end." (This idea, like references to "prime," anticipates the central issues of *The Prime of Miss Jean Brodie*, the novel that followed *Memento Mori*.) Here is a kind of renunciation of sin, the deception she has abetted. It is also a means of freeing both Charmian and Godfrey, so that they may give more attention to remembering death. As long as someone is obsessed with failure and reputation, he lacks openness to God's Will.

The futility of excessive concern with control is reiterated not only when Alec Warner's research records are all lost in the fire, but also in the final working out of wills. Lisa Brooke's inheritance goes not to Guy Leet as expected, but to an earlier lost husband, Matthew O'Brien, a gentle man who has been insane for years and who thinks he is God. Then he dies, and the scheming Mrs. Pettigrew finally is "rewarded" with the fortune she coveted. Over and over, the details in *Memento Mori* indicate how finite is man's capacity to know and control. Thus the wise and virtuous course is Jean Taylor's: an acceptance of God's Will, a transformation of whatever happens "to magnify the Lord." Muriel Spark not only argues the point through the characters and events, she also includes some explicit comments: "offered up to the Lord to whom no gift whatsoever is unacceptable" and "her spirit returned to God who gave it." Thus the novelist shows respect for the dignity of the individual soul, and this mitigates the stark view of decrepitude.

The strength of the novel lies, then, in its firm presentation of fundamental truths about the nature of man who lives in this world but more importantly, will live in the next. Perhaps *Memento Mori* has not been Spark's most popular novel because many readers share Alec Warner's response to Jean Taylor: "The more religious people are, the more perplexing I find them." Further, although the novel uses two familiar literary traditions—the suspense techniques of the modern detective story and the asperity of satire that is almost Swiftian—it also employs allegory, which is more difficult to understand. Death actually is a character in the novel, and the other characters, although remarkably particularized, are essentially types.

The telephone call is Spark's modernization of an old popular tradition. *Memento mori* means "remember you will die." During the Middle Ages and early Renaissance, there were powerful artistic representations of this idea to assure a constant awareness of mortality.[1] The west fronts of many medieval cathedrals were decorated with sculptures of the Last Judgment, and walls of churches were frequently covered with Doomsday paintings. Also notable was the Dance of Death, a figural representation in which a skeletal figure confronts people from all walks of life—knight, peasant, lady, bishop, king, pope—and all ages. The borders of Books of Hours were filled with these scenes in the Hours of the Dead, and great artists like Hans Holbein and Albrecht Durer in the sixteenth century made woodcut scenes of the Dance of Death. The morality play *Everyman* was a theatrical way of showing the same idea: Death comes to Everyman to summon him; Everyman realizes how little that he has thought important during his life on earth (the possessions and activities to which he has devoted himself) is actually important when he has to face God in eternity. There are many powerful and sobering presentations of the *memento mori* theme in earlier art, and Spark's novel is the finest contemporary expression of the idea.

Death is not a favorite subject; indeed it is often avoided in the modern world. Significantly, one of the epigrams that Spark used to preface *Memento Mori* comes from the penny cathechism. The question is: "What are the four last things to be ever remembered?" And the answer is: "Death, Judgment, Hell, and Heaven." After the Renaissance, there was a marked absence of consideration of the Four Last Things, and with the eighteenth century, "the age of reason and enlightenment," the emphasis was all upon man's capacity and achievement. Western attitudes toward Death changed markedly.[2] There was no longer the medieval and early Renaissance view of man's life on earth as a preparation for life in eternity but rather the idea of Death as the enemy, the Ravisher. Spark's brilliant achievement was to revitalize an earlier convention in a modern form, to treat a serious philosophical question with liveliness, to handle a macabre subject with a comic skill that dispels morbidity. She was to produce many other splendid novels, but none more impressive and distinctive.

5

Poems, Plays, and Stories

Muriel Spark's fame rightly comes from her novels, but she has also written some excellent poetry, several experimental plays, a large volume of short stories, and one children's book. However different the forms, the wit and style are unmistakably Sparkian, as are the exploitation of startling and bizarre situations and a characteristic concern with truth, reality, and religion.

Most of Spark's early work was poetry, and she still regularly publishes poems. Written in diverse forms, *Collected Poems I* included everything from a reworking of traditional children's verse in "The Grave that Time Dug" (a dark adaptation of "The House that Jack Built") to "Conundrum" (in the manner of Edward Lear's *Book of Nonsense*) to "Elegy in a Kensington Churchyard" (echoing the eighteenth-century Thomas Gray's "Elegy Written in a Country Churchyard") to translations from the Latin of Horace and Catullus.

Perhaps the most explicit statement of Spark's early interests came in "Against the Transcendentalists" in which she asked,

> Who is Everyman, what is he
> That he should stand in lieu of
> A poem? What is truth true of?
> And what good's a God's-eye-view of
> Anyone to anyone
> But God?

In this poem, Spark identifies poetry as the rarest commodity, but she rejects the romantic excesses often associated with it. This poet's place is Kensington, in contemporary and mundane London, not Byzantium, symbol of art for W. B. Yeats. Spark sought the human, stressing the importance of charity. The last line of "Against the Transcendentalists" is "The flesh made word," an inversion of the doctrine of the Incarnation of Christ ("The Word made flesh") that argues the centrality of art.

"The Nativity" contains four "conversations"—of the three wise men, of the shepherds, at the inn, and of the angels. Influenced by T. S. Eliot's "The Journey of the Magi," Spark's meditation upon the birth of Christ proclaimed the "common uncommonness" of man before the face of Christ. The distinctive voices and original articulation made this one of Spark's most memorable early poems. Her fascination with the birth of Christ was expressed again in "Three Kings." This is one of five poems published after the *Collected Poems I* (1967) and included in *Going up to Sotheby's,* a paperback edition printed in 1982.

Many poems included in *Collected Poems I* showed a fine ear for voices and verbal dexterity, though not all anticipate Spark's major themes in the novels. Some, like "A Tour of London" and "Edinburgh Villanella," are observations about places. "Bluebell among the Sables" is about a cat, a deliciously satiric comment about pretension and an argument for living creatures. "A Visit" is quite surrealist: a steel chair meets a cabinet, and there is a dancing girl whose breasts are alarm clocks. Spark made the bizarre vivid through clear and concise dialogue. Frequent use of voices and dramatic scenes, as well as the emerging Christian statements, anticipated the major work.

Spark's most ambitious poem is "The Ballad of the Fanfarlo." About the same length as T. S. Eliot's *The Waste Land*, it begins with the ballad style of the Scots borders and gradually introduces echoes of nearly all the great English poets. The prefatory epigram comes from a short story "La Fanfarlo" by Baudelaire, who reacted strongly against romanticism. Using the character Samuel Cramer as protagonist, Spark examined the romantic cast of mind and the self-indulgent assertive personality it assumes—an idea later fully explored in Jean Brodie. Cramer tells lies, making claims about a friend and a mistress to mask his emptiness. The romantic finds himself in "No-Man's sanitorium," a place with conflict and fierce claims for personal ego. Cramer meets Death—an anticipation of *Memento Mori* that even includes the line, "Will you remember me?" He wants "A way to depart in peace," and neither friend Manuela nor mistress Fanfarlo—romantic ideas made into character—can answer. Death is able to offer only "a proper mortality," "a staple amnesia." Cramer believes that he can "hack his way to the bounds of Heaven and Hell." Spark constantly decried the romantic exaltation of personality, and here she showed Cramer rejecting the Christian solution because he cannot contemplate loss of his active self, the phenomena of the world. A "steel chair," which suggests modern impersonality and simple reliance on facts, is a principal spokesman. The Christian extinction of self to realize peace is not acceptable to the romantic egoist.

Like Spark's fiction, "The Ballad of the Fanfarlo" was both humorous and provocatively serious. Thematic interest was carried over through Samuel Cramer, who was also the protagonist of Spark's first short story "The Seraph and the Zambesi," which won *The Observer* competition in 1951. Remarkably masterful and original, the story continued Spark's investigation of the romantic egoist and the supernatural. Baudelaire's half-poet, half-journalist was modified into a sometime writer and keeper of a petrol pump near the Zambesi River.

The year is 1946, and Cramer's nativity masque is performed on Christmas Eve in his garage. In the midst of the performance, the narrator is aware of great heat coming from "a living body," and "unlike other forms of life, it had a completed look." Having interrupted the masque, the Seraph identifies itself and quietly explains the show has been his "from the Beginning" and he will not let Cramer go on. Furious at the displacement of his art, Cramer orders the troopers to burn the building with petrol. As the Seraph warns, the fire is intense and Cramer's garage destroyed. Cramer, of course, is insured against "everything except Acts of God." The narrator by the glare of the headlights sees the Seraph "going at about seventy miles an hour and skimming the tarmac strips with two of his six wings in swift motion, two folded over his face, and two covering his feet." They go into the Rain Forest and watch the Seraph "ride the Zambesi away from us."

This story is one of several that used an African setting, made vivid through Spark's precise description and the measured speech of colonial boredom and disorientation. Among the best was "Bang-bang, You're Dead," an account of a shooting in which the wrong woman is killed. The heroine Sybil looks at films made eighteen years earlier and recalls her association with Désirée, her twin in appearance but her opposite in temperament. Sybil, whose name suggests the knowledge of the oracle, is superior intellectually and very much a person apart. She marries but is soon bored by her husband, since she, unlike other women, wants to be married to a "Mind." Thus she is relieved when he is killed by a lion in the second year of their marriage. Sybil is uninterested in men; only "in a frenzy of self-discipline" can she become carnally excited. Désirée, in contrast, embodies sensuousness and constantly chides Sybil about needing a man. Sybil has a brief affair with David, whom everyone describes as in love with Désirée. The rejected lover shoots not Sybil but Désirée, whom he mistakes for Sybil. The superior intellect observes and notes, but feels little. The story concludes with Sybil's calmly asking the question, "Am I a woman, or an intellectual monster?"

Another similar heroine is Needle in "The Portobello Road," a story that moves from Africa to London. The narrator is a ghost come back to haunt her murderer George, who killed her to stop her telling a friend Kathleen about his marriage to a black woman in Africa. Much is made of the "luck" of Needle, whose name comes from her finding the proverbial needle in a haystack, which is also where she was choked in the hay.

"The Go-Away Bird," title story of Spark's first collection of stories and the longest in *Collected Stories I*, directly addresses the relationship between England and the colony. Daphne is eager to leave Africa, to study and live in green England. A precocious child, she understands the long feud between Chakata, her uncle, and Old Tuys, the manager whom Chakata must, in honor, keep on at the tobacco farm. Daphne wants to experience a richer life, and "The Go-Away Bird" describes her many encounters and disillusionments. The Second World War delays her going to England, and after a time family responsibility makes her return to Africa from London. Old Tuys murders her, shooting her like an animal, in revenge against Chakata who had been his wife's lover. Ralph Mercer, a novelist who has been Daphne's lover in England, goes to Africa to try to make sense of the tragedy. Here Spark again evoked a feeling of Africa, especially the prejudices and the class expectations that circumscribe colonial life. The title describes the call of an African bird, the grey-crested Lourie, and this is a refrain throughout the narrative.

A specifically Catholic interest is recorded in stories

like "The Black Madonna" and "Come Along, Marjorie." Both are sharply critical of Catholics of a particular kind. The first tells of a liberal Catholic white couple who have a black baby, a child born after their prayers to the Black Madonna, a statue made from bog oak. Lou and Raymond, the couple, are appalled, not appreciating the miracle nor accepting the idea that the Catholic Christian can expect to suffer. Living by one's beliefs is, then, not easy.

The demands of Christian community are considered in "Come Along, Marjorie," a story set at Watling Abbey, where "pilgrims" go to recover or at least ease their nervous conditions. The narrator calls herself Gloria Deplores-you, a name that richly suggests the character of the woman whose religious understanding is very different from that of the others at the Abbey. Gloria is alienated by the social demands of the group, though they have in common Catholicism. The exception is the character of the title. Known to the group as Miss Marjorie Pettigrew, this shy and silent woman resists all urging to communicate with others. She keeps her solitude, goes to confession and Mass, and fasts. Then people come to take her to an asylum and call her "Marjorie." Thus neat, quiet, reserved Miss Pettigrew is diminished by casual familiarity. What else can be done with someone who has "foolish medieval ideas" and speaks only once, to Gloria, to give the message "The Lord is risen"?

Collected Stories I brought together the early collections, *The Go-Away Bird* and *Voices at Play*, and also included two other stories originally published in *The New Yorker*.[1] The brevity of the short story fosters a single tone and attitude, and Spark recognized a unity in various forms that she was using at this time. The 1961 volume *Voices at Play* contained four radio plays, written for the "Third Programme" of the BBC, and six short stories. In an author's note, Spark explained:

"two different forms of writing . . . were written on the same creative wavelength. The plays were written for the outward ear, and the stories for the inward ear." Thus plays and stories showed a consistent mood, and long sections of dialogue in the stories sounded very much like the plays.

The Danger Zone, the longest and most challenging play, is subtitled "An elemental drama." It contains eleven scenes and three settings—The Valley, The Mountain Side, and The Mountain Top—which are in Wales but also not "quite in Wales." Fourteen characters are equally divided into adults and young people, sharply differentiated groups. The older generation lives in The Valley and are first heard with tinkling glasses expressing dismay that their children use their spare time, Friday evenings and Sunday afternoons, to go up the mountain. All the youngsters from the age of sixteen are different, for they see things that others do not see. The signs are very clear: their voices are foreign and their eyes become slitlike. Parents note that their children avoid the dance hall, ignore material goods like a beautiful record player, and speak of a "danger" on the mountain. The Reverend Hugh Pugh, father of Thomas, observes, "The age of sixteen is a strange sort of age. Sixteen—one-six. Six and one make seven. Seven is a mystical number."

Spark's play was, then, basically an allegory about the way of life that one chooses. The youngsters who meet on the mountainside judge their elders to be "childish," if not mad. All are concerned with the material quality of life—washing machine, telephone, car, television—and can imagine only that their children go away for sex. The voices of the adults are always accompanied by the sound of glasses and bottles of the local mineral water that they drink to ease the pain of their lives. Reverend Pugh takes only half a glass, while others consume in quantity. He wants to "cross the border that stands between" the generations; thus he goes to the mountainside.

The spokesman for the young people is Jones, son of Richard Jones, a bachelor craftsman who believed "an abstemious life was necessary to the craftsman," until his work was rejected by the world as "Not fundamental enough in the design." Jones has a special affinity for an otherworldly life; thus he is trying to hold back the Danger of those over the mountain who may come too soon. When Danger-Boy asks for mineral water, Jones refuses him, and he also warns Pugh. But the minister drinks the mineral water that brings madness to those in the valley. Then Pugh goes up the mountain to join the community of youngsters at their campfire and there meets the Danger-Boy.

The view from the Mountain Top is "the real Wales *sub specie aeternitatis.*" In Pugh, Danger-Boy gets the hostage he demanded, in spite of Jones's efforts to protect the reverend, but Danger-Boy's repeated demand for mineral water is still refused. Pugh is at last told "the rules of the game," and he is startled to learn from Jones that they are: "Poverty, Chastity, Obedience. And no taking of mineral water or inciting others to it." Danger-Boy, of course, still wants to become like the adults in the Valley and does not choose Jones' alternative abstention.

When Jones meets Danger-Boy again, demands for mineral water are intensified, for the minister has described its exciting properties. Jones refuses, asking, "Do you want to become like the people of the old world—money, comfort, success, lust, self-indulgence . . . ?" He concludes that Pugh has made Danger-Boy "mad." In fact, Pugh is killed, his blood drunk, and Danger-Boy and the others come down from the mountain to drink mineral water from the stream. In the final scene, Danger-Boy is so completely assimilated by the oldsters that he can scarcely remember his other life.

"Poverty, Chastity, Obedience"—the vows of religious life—are contemptuously dismissed as unrewarding. Forgetting troubles by drinking is preferred to self-discipline and self-denial. *The Danger Zone* is, then, that area into which people stray as they are trying to decide how to live their lives. The play is a kind of meditation on the difficulty of seeking and realizing a religious life amidst the materialism and evasiveness of worldly existence.

The other plays in *Voices at Play* all involve ghosts and contain hallucinatory effects. *The Dry Bed* is set in South Africa and reflects racial tensions. It also explores further differences in the points of view of older and younger generations, here the colonials. A murder and attempted murder are counterpointed with the casual conversation of women who are having tea. The party in question in *The Party through the Wall* occurred long ago in the rooms of a countess who had heard Lizst perform. Ethel Carson, who is troubled by nerves, hears the party in contemporary London. A narrator, who is subsequently identified as the psychologist Dr. Fell, explains. He is interested in exceptional cases, specifically those who are haunted by the ghost of the sister he strangled fifty years ago. He is "sensitive to the life of the spirit around us" and glad to have Miss Carson move away, because "she was getting frightfully on my nerves."

In *The Interview*, Dame Lettice Chatterton, a political activist of the twenties, writes her memoirs while her secretary is reciting facts learned for a quiz competition. Their conversations are interrupted by appearances of Dame Lettice's nephew Roy, who experiments with many styles of life—witchcraft, Roman Catholicism, communism, smuggling. In the last encounter, Roy explains that he intends to marry Tiggy, the secretary. Suddenly they realize that they "can see right through Roy"—a typical Spark pun—for he explains that ten minutes ago he was killed in a plane crash. The theme of *The Interview* is given in the completed line of Dame Lettice's autobiography: "If these memoirs prove anything at all, they prove the supremacy of the world of imagination, a world in which literally anything can happen, over the mundane facts of everyday life."

Spark's many explorations of the relation between mystery and rationalism, the value of different kinds of being and doing, indicated both preoccupation with these themes and a concern to advocate a wider tolerance. It was, then, not surprising that she treated the same idea in a children's book, *The Very Fine Clock*. Children's literature characteristically reflects the interest and values of the adult society that produces it and influences the shaping of the next generation. *The Very Fine Clock,* through a simple parable, makes the same judgment that is found in the sophisticated and witty play *Doctors of Philosophy*.

Ticky is one of many clocks owned by Professor Horace John Morris, and each night Professor John sets all the other timepieces by Ticky's time. Every Thursday night, four other professors, all "clever and famous" men, come to talk. One Thursday they discuss the favorite clock's importance in providing the exact time and decide that, because of his wisdom, the clock should be "Professor Ticky." Ticky, however, refuses this distinction because he fears it would cost him the friendship of the other clocks who would think him too grand. The professors are impressed by Ticky's nobility: charity is more esteemed than assertion of intellectual superiority. Ticky explains that he talks to the professors on the one evening, but during the days he tells stories with all the other clocks. Ticky values each for its special characteristics, particularly Pepita in the spare room. She can say only "Ticky, Ticky, Ticky," not "professor." Thus Spark reaffirmed a belief in the importance of community, an awareness of something beyond self-interest, and noted the limits of intellectual life.

A more sophisticated investigation of the academic was Muriel Spark's stage play, *Doctors of Philosophy*. Produced in London in 1962, the play is a fascinating experiment with the conventions of the theater that is probably more effective when read than seen. It breaks down ordinary views of reality, the traditional objective of philosophical questioning. Speculation becomes concrete when actors move parts of the stage setting to break the illusion of the theatre. Three of the principals, a man and two women, are Ph.D.s—appropriate figures to question the nature of reality.

The play is set in the Delfonts' house, which overlooks the Regent's Canal. The men are all called Charlie, and this suggests that they are somewhat incidental and interchangeable. Interest centers upon the women. Two of the women are cousins and their lives are contrasted. Catherine, after receiving a brilliant degree at Oxford, married Charlie Delfont, an economist who has just been made a professor. She has not pursued an academic career, but rather been a wife and mother and a teacher at the local grammar school—though her husband belittles this. She resents receiving nightdresses rather than books for her birthday and believes she could still be a first-rate scholar, but lacks "the solitude and the freedom, and the leisure." Leonora chose the opposite way; she is a don at Oxford, a classicist who has a scholarly reputation but has never married. The two women visit regularly and constantly air their jealous rivalry.

A third woman, Annie Wood, is also a cousin of Catherine. Lacking a Ph.D., she identifies the others as "Doctors of Philosophy, every one of them. They live such dignified lives, my dears. They have stately conversations with each other. They never have to take pep-up pills or keep-calm pills. Philosophers, that's what they are." However, the supposed peace of the Delfont household is only an illusion.

Catherine thinks that Leonora needs to "take a look at reality" during the vacation, instead of seeing things as ideas. Leonora becomes elemental when she approaches Charlie Delfont with the request "give me a child." This concern seems unreal in a university teacher committed to an ideal of celibacy as essential for the scholar; her subject is Greek, not life force. Leonora has spent two years working on a scholarly problem about Assyria; an unexpected find of tablets "blows" all her theories. In short, Leonora finds herself in a completely different situation, and Catherine's comment about her high standards and remote life seems pertinent: "Reality forces one to lower one's standards."

Hearing her own voice on the tape recorder is a kind of revelation for Leonora, who recognizes that emotions require as much attention as ideas and are as worthy of analysis. She thinks that she may be having a nervous breakdown, but an analyst would not help because he would be less intelligent than she. Leonora admits that "Reality is very alarming at first and then it becomes interesting." She finds herself in a new dramatic role, and she acts: "I've done something with my life for the first time in my life." She accepts the offer of a four-year lectureship at Columbia, where she will also again see an American professor with whom she was "rather thick."

Catherine, whose role in life is the reverse of Leonora's, also changes dramatically. For all her concentration on the family situation, Catherine has longed to develop ideas about the ancient past rather than an understanding of her emotional present. Her daughter Daphne's pregnancy and refusal to marry young Charlie Weston—whom she loves but must reject philosophically since he is a nuclear researcher and she a political activist against atomic proliferation—are a reality that Catherine must cope with. Like Leonora, she acts. With the help of a lorry driver, Charlie Brown, Catherine stages a suicide attempt and rescue for young Charlie Weston. Confronted with the apparent reality of losing the man she loves, Daphne deserts the reality of her idea about how to behave. The lovers are reunited and their child has a future with the two of them. "Dramatic realism" serves Catherine well; she has "made a brilliant start." Through her intelligence, Catherine has arranged a solution; not academic ideas, but life triumphs.

Flexibility and resilience are constantly expressed by Annie Wood, "a very religious type," "always prepared for things I'm unprepared for," and suitably dressed for every occasion. The two brilliant cousins do not understand reality, for they have assumed rigidly fixed points. The dramatic action in *Doctors of Philosophy* involves not only a growing understanding of the complexities of human behavior but also the corollary need for a principle based on something beyond reality as it is perceived in the world.

Leonora describes herself in a play context; she feels observed by an invisible audience, and she recognizes that "the scenery is unreliable." Intellectual assumptions are not always supported solidly. Thus, when Mrs. Weston charges, "You scholars are not realists," Leonora follows Annie's injunction and pushes the wall. And all the spaces are changed, for "Realism is very flimsy." Leonora's new start in America is promising; it is a deliberate reshaping of her life that will prevent the nervous breakdown that is imminent. Annie's wisdom is not quite in the grasp of the Doctors of Philosophy, but the rational people are now nearer to realizing "that there's a mysterious force that provides for the needs of simple-minded ordinary women."

An interesting link between the world of intellect and ordinariness is the daily help, Mrs. S., who has been with the Delfonts for six years. She is wary: "I wouldn't trust an eleven-plus never mind a Ph.D."[2] Her sharp, deflating remarks provide much of the comedy in *Doctors of Philosophy*. Mrs. S. comments about the parents' unawareness of their daughter's pregnancy: "They are deep thinkers, my dear, not common detectives. Doctors of philosophy, not medicine. Must a happened at Oxford." She knows everything that is going on in the house, even though she constantly recites factual information and cites academic authorities. Mrs. S. neatly imitates, but she is never earnest. Asked by Charlie the lorry driver whether the Delfonts have read all their books, she replies, "They don't use them for reading, they are educated people, they refer to them." She can make light of having a nervous breakdown: "Yes. I shall never forget. I had it on a Tuesday afternoon in March a few years ago. . . ." and parody romantic posturing. Mrs. S. calls herself a scholar, but she does not suffer from the "inconsistencies of attitude in the private life," the saying of "what one doesn't mean in one's own house," that characterize intellectuals. She ferrets out information, reels off facts, but uses this knowledge directly to improve the quality of life not as diverting abstract thinking.

The lorry driver Charlie Brown shares Mrs. S.'s directness. He warns, "You can't judge by appearances," but he follows the instinctual suggestions of the women, whether in helping with the pretended suicide or in deciding to marry the widow who "wanted him." As Annie tells Charlie, "It's a woman's world when all is said and done." This recognition of women's strength comes from their role as the weaker sex. Knowing one's limitations eliminates delusions about relying upon a purely rational way of living, traditionally the masculine ideal. To be merely reasonable leads to a nervous breakdown. "One must look for supernatural means."

The supernatural was always familiar in Spark's work, but in three novels published between 1960 and 1963, the date of *Doctors of Philosophy*, she seemed to concentrate her attention upon manifestations of the supernatural and divergent responses to it in the material world. Spark's poems, plays, and short stories provide a memorable exploration of the ideas with which she was most concerned in a different, and often simpler, form. The short novel best suited her talent, and she effectively and characteristically used it, almost exclusively, as a fully mature artist. Spark, however, never simply repeats but always stretches and creates new directions for the favored form, to which we now return.

6

Singles in London

The Ballad of Peckham Rye

To follow *Memento Mori* with *The Ballad of Peckham Rye* is to go from brilliant achievement to respectable work. The title of Muriel Spark's fourth novel suggests the "something light and lyrical" that she needed as a respite.[1] A ballad is a short narrative that relies heavily on dialogue to make a simple statement, without great emotion, of what happened. Originally songs, ballads often have as their subject a tragic event (often a murder) and involve the supernatural. In *The Ballad of Peckham Rye* Spark playfully explored such artistic possibilities, imitating the detached tone of a balladeer who chronicles cruelty but allows grim humor.

Dougal Douglas, an Arts graduate from Edinburgh, goes to Peckham Rye, where Mr. R. V. Druce hires him as assistant to Mr. Weedin, Personnel Manager of Meadows, Meade & Grindley, manufacturers of nylon textiles. Dougal's task is "to bring vision into the lives of the workers." Industry is to be vitalized by alleviating absenteeism. Declaring, "It will be my job to take the pulse of the people and to plumb the industrial depths of Peckham," Dougal sets about with great energy. He meets and mingles with the workers, involves himself in their lives and freely gives advice.

He secures a second job, as Douglas Dougal, with the town's rival textile firm, Drover Willis, again as a researcher with much free time. He investigates both the present environment and the past history, including the city's archeological explorations, for he argues, "Peckham must have a moral character of its own." Dougal Douglas also works as a writer, composing the autobiography of an aging actress, Maria Cheeseman. As a "crooked ghost," he gives her a lively childhood in Peckham—though she actually lived in Streatham. The creation of this work of art, he insists, is taking all his time.

This central character is more than a man who holds several jobs. He is given the attributes of the devil, a description that is reinforced by the confusions and final horror, a murder, that he brings into the lives of those he meets. Dougal's appearance is crooked; his right shoulder is higher than his left. He also has two little bumps on his head, left by the plastic surgeon when he had an operation to take away the two horns. Described as a "succubus," Dougal is regarded by some as a devil or diabolic agent, and he appears in his own dream as the devil. He calls himself "one of the wicked spirits that wander through the world for the ruin of souls," but he also claims "powers of exorcism, the ability to drive devils out of people." In one scene he poses as an angel-devil on a tombstone, an iconographically important moment, since Dougal Douglas is a good-bad character.

Spark creates a mystery, for her central character is a shape shifter. Constantly adapting his manner and appearance, choosing the role that pleases or startles, Dougal, through "human research," causes Peckham's inhabitants to intensify and isolate their inherent traits. A releaser of controlled behavior, he is a catalyst who alters people's attention and often their actions. He declares that "we all have a fatal flaw" and seeks this in everyone.

Peckham's pervasive drabness of life is most obviously expressed in the relationship of Merle Cover-
dale, head of the typing pool, and Mr. Druce. Both
Merle's employer and her lover, Druce has not spoken
to his wife for five years, since the Sunday lunch when
she interrupted him with "Quack, quack . . . Quack,
quack." But Druce is bound to Merle only by habit;
the description of their sexual encounter, with its unfeeling tedium, echoes T. S. Eliot's *The Waste Land.*
This quality is not abated even when Druce routinely
murders Merle with a corkscrew.

The sterility of Peckham Rye is also found in Joyce
Willis, the snobbish middle class wife of Richard,
manager of Drover Willis. Constantly chattering—her
conversation is punctuated with the phrase "quite
frankly"—this childless woman sees Douglas as a
surrogate son, an aid that will offset the dominance of
her husband's partner in the expanding firm.

The Ballad of Peckham Rye begins and ends with
the marriage of Dixie and Humphrey Place, but again
the union is unfeeling. As in a ballad, the townspeople
tell the story without remembering details except that
the groom said "No" at the altar. Asked if he would
have the woman to wife, Humphrey actually said,
"No, to be quite frank I won't." Influenced by
Douglas, he is trying to avoid the stale entrapment of
marriage to a penny-pinching woman with an all-
consuming desire for money. Since she defines
marriage as "acquiring things," Dixie has lost her
sexual interest. Two months after the initial rejection
Humphrey retreats from his assertive frankness,
marries Dixie, and is merely saddened to hear her say
that she feels that she has been married twenty years,
not two hours. As they drive on, he sees "the Rye for an
instant looking like a cloud of green and gold, the
people seeming to ride upon it, as you might say there
was another world than this."

The image of the Rye, a beautiful and lush land-

scape, is always at the edge of the industrial center of
Peckham. Spark uses "the Rye's broad lyrical acres" to
suggest the disharmony between the novel's commonplaces and potential transcendence. Dougal observes to Mr. Druce, "Vision is the first requisite of
sanity." He also notes that "the moral element lay at
the root of all industrial discontents." Then he
elaborates the four types of morality observable in
Peckham: emotional, functional, puritanical,
Christian. These are illustrated as: separating from a
wife who no longer appeals, class solidarity as in the
trade union movement, monetary advancement, and
traditional. The last category, which is simply
Christian, accounts for only about one percent of the
population.

That one percent appears in the person of Nelly
Mahone, "who had lapsed from her native religion on
religious grounds." Regularly seen at a pub and often
mistaken for a drunken woman, Nelly is the one individual who praises God, "whose ancient miracles we
see shining in our times." Inhabitants of Peckham Rye
do not even recall the town's recent history. Nellie
believes in "the glory of the faithful and the life of the
just." She provides criteria for evaluating Dougal
when she names the

Six things . . . which the Lord hateth, and the seventh his
soul detesteth. Haughty eyes, a lying tongue, hands that
shed innocent blood. . . . A heart that deviseth wicked plots,
feet that are swift to run into mischief. . . . A deceitful witness that uttereth lies. . . . And him that soweth discord
among brethren.

This list of charges is easily proved against Dougal
Douglas.

Spark delights in speculation about the supernatural, never more than in the diabolic associations of
the central character, whose manipulative successes
are fascinating and awesome. Each offense hated by

the Lord is, however, a common human failing; evil
triumphs because humans choose it. Dougal Douglas is
a superlative actor, a player of many roles, and a ghost
writer, a creator of fantasy lives for those caught in
torpid existence.

Peckham Rye's inhabitants find his virtuosity
irresistible; it distracts them from their own fatal
flaws—meaningless sexuality, denial of a lost brother
in need, blackmail, jealousy, violence. Because
Peckham's inhabitants lack discernment and concentrate only on self, Dougal can break their nerve.
Insecure about his position, Mr. Weedin is reduced to
tears and then fury, restrained only because the office
walls are made of glass. Trevor Lomas is less controlled. An electrician, he is Humphrey's best friend
and has a girl friend called Beauty. Trevor resents
both Dougal's artistic sensibility and the attention he
attracts. At first meeting, Trevor mocks Dougal's tears
over losing a girl; he later conspires against Dougal,
whom he regards as an intruder, and finally attacks
him with intent to kill. This happens as Dougal is
leaving Peckham through the tunnel just finished for
archeological investigation. It is an echo of the climax
of *Robinson*, which also occurs in a tunnel.

The only person unaffected by the devilish Dougal is
Elaine Kent. She is "well on in her twenties, an experienced controller of process," and thus more com-
manding than those who are influenced by emotion.
She soothes Dougal, enjoys his company, cautions
against fighting. In the midst of the street fight, Elaine
cleverly alerts and shifts the crowd—who could not
resist a melée—when she sees the police approaching.
Elaine remains detached, free from nerves and un-
touched by Dougal's psychological pressures, though
amused and interested. Elaine laughs uproariously at
his wildly abandoned dancing and mimicry, and she
prevents fights, for a time, by pointing out that he is
"deformed." Elaine recognizes that Dougal is "dif-

ferent," and even notes a Celtic kinship, through his being Scots and her having an Irish mother. She knows that Dougal Douglas is up to some game, but she does not interfere. She compromises by calling him "Doug," a nickname that is noncommittal, since it serves for Dougal Douglas or Douglas Dougal.

Her attitude is similar to that of Nelly, who insists, even when she is threatened by Trevor, that Dougal's activities are "only his larks. He's off his nut."

In addition to their cognizance of Dougal Douglas's character, Elaine and Nelly also share a wish for peace and a concern for others' well-being. This is in sharp contrast with Dougal's fatal flaw; he cannot bear illness, "anyone off colour." He simply abandons all associations when there is a hint that anything may be asked of him. Evil here may be defined as the One's refusal to recognize the Other; and, when the One does recognize the Other, evil is avoidable.

When Peckham Rye is finally rid of Dougal, he goes to Africa to sell tape-recorders to witch doctors. This is a typical Spark detail, a grotesque way of noting that the products of industrialization will spread into the jungle. From this adventure Dougal proceeds to a Franciscan monastery as a novice. Only after "the Prior had endured a nervous breakdown" and several monks had broken their vows was he asked to leave. Part of that one percent who live according to religious, traditional morality, act effectively: they reject the devil. "Thereafter, for economy's sake, he gathered the scrap ends of the profligate experience—for he was a frugal man at heart—and turned them into a lot of cockeyed books, and went far in the world."

Creating plots and manipulating characters in books may be worrying, but it is not evil like causing death and breakdowns. The novel *The Ballad of Peckham Rye* is fiction, not life. Spark described her work as "a collection of lies from which emerges a kind of truth."[2] A temporary abatement of evil comes when Dougal leaves Peckham; the making of fiction serves as Spark's banishment of devils. Her analysis, presented here with outrageous and grotesque humor, leads to thoughtful speculations, as well as hilarity and rueful recognition.

The Bachelors

Written in the same year as *The Ballad of Peckham Rye*, *The Bachelors* is set in "the metropolitan city" London and explores ideas of community, the individual's isolation, and the role of the novelist. There are splended comic moments, but *The Bachelors* is a very serious novel. The dominant impression is of philosophical and theological investigation through meticulously detailed and cogently selected naturalistic scenes and characters. While *The Ballad of Peckham Rye* is ambiguous, *The Bachelors* is explicit; the mystery and speculations provoked in Spark's first novels are here replaced by certainties and control.

Muriel Spark again focused on a specific group—bachelors, largely professional, who live in middle-class Chelsea, Kensington, and Hampstead. The plot springs from Patrick Seton, a spiritualist with a long criminal record of blackmail, fraud, and exploitation of foolish women. Ronald Bridges, a handwriting expert, is a principal witness for the prosecution at Seton's trial for improper acquisition of money from a doting admirer. Ronald, who is the real center of *The Bachelors*, carelessly talks about the letter that is the evidence against Seton. The letter is stolen, and there is some suspense about its recovery. Further tension comes from Patrick's plan to murder his mistress after the trial, which he expects will end in his favor. In this narrative of mystery, Spark in-

troduced a memorably precise delineation of city life
and an extraordinary group of characters.

On an elementary level, the novel is restricted to one
kind of person, and there is an unusual focus on male
characters: "I wrote a book about bachelors and it
seemed to me that everyone was a bachelor."[2] Included are eleven unmarried men, three single girls,
two widows, and a divorcée. Some are paired, but
most are physically alone, and all remain isolated
because of never really sharing, even when lives are
linked through encounters, plots, and deceptions.
Separate   loneliness   is   eschewed: "There's   no
justification for being a bachelor and that's the truth,
let's face it. It's everyone's duty to be fruitful and
multiply according to his calling either spiritual or
temporal, as the case may be."

An acceptance of spiritual and temporal is fundamental to Spark's investigation of reality in *The
Bachelors*. Her exploration of the religious dimension
of being centers on solipsism. As a bachelor defines
reality exclusively in terms of the self, admitting only
his own perception, so those without religious belief
refuse to recognize anything beyond the present
moment. And "The truth is, a married man is
psychologically stronger." Similarly, without a unity
of being—God, nature, community—"It is all
demonology and to do with creatures of the air." This
is the judgment of the central figure in the novel, one
whose name itself (Bridges) suggests the necessity of
uniting the disparate.

Ronald Bridges is Spark's persona in *The Bachelors*.
A thirty-seven-year-old, whose epilepsy is a "voca-
tion," he is perceptive, analytical, and detached.
The infirmity that prevented his becoming a Roman
Catholic priest, has provided Ronald with a
knowledge of his own limitations that deeply influences his judgment of human behavior. Ancient

superstitions surround "the falling sickness," "the sacred disease," "the evil spirit." Ronald's acquaintances patronize and fuss about his illness, making him feel like "a sacred cow" or "a wise monkey." However, in crises, they expect him to be "a kind of truth machine" and thus appear to him as "demon-hypocrites." A graphologist, Ronald offers expert opinion about forgeries, identifying truth or falsity. His professional analysis of handwritten documents brings him to the trial of Patrick Seton.

This fifty-five-year-old medium is accused of taking money from Freda Flower under false pretenses. Ronald is asked to evaluate a letter to Patrick offering Freda's admiration and £ 2000 "to further your psychic and spiritual work." Seton, whose name might be pronounced Satan, is so effective at seances that his authenticity as a medium is never doubted, even by his detractors. He has loyal supporters, some solicited by Marlene Cooper, a widow under whose patronage he works. She believes so ardently in her dead husband's spirit that she must summon him from the grave. She sponsors two spiritualist groups—a large one called Wider Infinity and the smaller Interior Spiral. Freda, who once was also Patrick's intimate, has become disaffected.

Patrick's current mistress is Alice Dawes, a "soul-lover" who believes in his innocence. Now pregnant, she urges marriage. For bachelor Patrick, whose entire life has been a flight from reality, an evasion of anything material, this is impossible. Saying that he must wait for a divorce, Patrick arranges to take Alice to Austria after the trial. She has refused to have an abortion, and Patrick plans to kill her by denying her the heavy insulin injections that her diabetic condition requires. Indeed, Patrick's defense at his trial rises to eloquent heights because of his recurrent vision of Alice's death. As he did all his previous criminal acts, he sees this as right because everything is only an extension of his own will. Thus even murder is allowable.

Patrick's spiritualism is without a moral dimension. His apparent otherworldliness is simply a mask, and he deceives many with his physical qualities—thin, pale, with fading voice. Patrick is a good medium—his trances are genuine, and he reveals some truths he does not consciously know—but he is a fraudulent human being. He suggests something beyond the temporal moment, then tries to impose his vision on the mystery. Spiritualism is not a true religion, because essentially it is a refusal to embrace the confines of the material world and to recognize mystery. Nothing can be left beyond human understanding. The spiritualist not only thinks that the dead are still alive; he believes they cannot "be left in the grave to rot."

In some ways Ronald Bridges closely resembles Patrick Seton. The physical signs of the medium's trances are exactly like those of Ronald's epilepsy, an analogy that is made explicit in the climactic trial scene. Having given his testimony, Ronald starts down the steps and then falls into a seizure. The judge asks, "Is this man a medium?" Certainly Ronald has understanding beyond the commonplaces of all his bachelor acquaintances. When he thinks back on an occasion like Isobel Billows' cocktail party, for example, it "storms upon him like a play." This visionary perception extends also to his seeing those who are near him as "a company of ridiculous demons."

If anything, Ronald's periodic "great melancholy boredom," "times of utter disenchantment," and "disgust," are more intense and frequent than Patrick's experiences. However, "the company of demons" that attack him in moments of despair, do not conquer. Ronald has disciplined himself to fend off such forces with "desperate acts of diligence," simply getting on with trivial details. He is also intellectually certain that "You never get all you want in life." Ronald's pessimism is a reasoned one. "It is better to be a pessimist in life, it makes life endurable. The slightest optimism invites disappointment." When "at times of utter disenchantment no distraction whatsoever prevails," the dilemma of how to go on living is resolved through Ronald's choice of religion.

At one point in *The Bachelors*, Ronald says, "There are only two religions, the spiritualist and the Catholic." In explicit contrast with Seton, Ronald is talking in a figurative sense. Roman Catholicism accepts the material; it admits the mundane, recognizing matter as part of God's creation, while many reject this in pursuit of otherworldliness. The Roman Catholics in *The Bachelors* are as sinful as others; Ronald observes, "The Christian economy seems to be so ordered that original sin is necessary to salvation." He is not pietistic. When asked how he feels about something "as a Catholic," Ronald turns in irritation: "As a Catholic I loathe all other Catholics." He shouts his resentment of the question because "To me, being Catholic is part of my human existence. I don't feel one way as a human being and another *as a Catholic.*"[3]

What this means in practical terms is that Ronald copes with melancholy and boredom by reciting a passage from St. Paul's Epistle to the Philippians (4:8):

> All that rings true, all that commands reverence, and all that makes for right; all that is pure, all that is lovely, all that is gracious in the telling; virtue and merit, wherever virtue and merit are found—let this be the argument of your thoughts.

The demons are exorcised when Ronald, having first admitted his own repulsiveness, lists his acquaintances and finds in each some merit or virtue. A "violent wrench of the mind" is necessary, and later Ronald has an epileptic seizure. This happens often after "he had made some effort of will towards graciousness, as if a

devil in his body was taking its revenge." This, too, he
accepts, going to confession not to be rid of the
thoughts, but "to receive, in absolution, a friendly
gesture of recognition from the maker of heaven and
earth, vigilant manipulator of the falling sickness."
Ronald's faith in God transcends the rituals of the
Church.

His role in *The Bachelors* is not only to profess this
belief, but also to live it. Ronald Bridges is set apart by
his epilepsy; but he remains human, a typological
representation of the Christian pilgrim on earth. He
could not bear the love of his mistress Hildegarde, an
"admirable" woman who "did everything for him"
and called him "a genius," thus indicating "not her
belief about his mental capacity but her secret belief in
the superiority of her own." He cannot abrogate his
own being and rejects anyone who tries to control.
Ronald makes mistakes: he talks to his friend Matthew
Finch about the document he is to evaluate for the
court. Finch then tells Alice, and her friend Elsie steals
the document, in the belief that this will protect Seton
and thus help Alice. Later when Ronald asks Elsie to
return the letter, she first refuses and then tries to
bargain. Elsie asks Ronald to give her something, to
stay the night. Elsie is overwhelmed with despair at
the sterility of her experience, for she resents having
sex with no relationship and finds contraceptives
distasteful. However, she seeks desperately to assuage
her loneliness. Ronald refuses Elsie's offer and instead
humbly asks her to give him the letter to save his
reputation, to set right his mistake. Against her
elemental wish for advantage and resentment about
being previously exploited, Ronald argues simply,
"Give it to me for love. . . . The best type of love to
give is superficial. It's an embarrassing type of love to
receive, if that's any consolation to you." He persists in
asking her to be "a dependable person and otherwise

ignored." Exhausted, Elsie says, "Christ! you're driving me mad." Of course, by her previous experience of the world, she does behave "madly"; she gives him the letter. In fact, Ronald has given Elsie what no man has previously offered—truth, respect, and the freedom to choose. The evidence of the forgery helps convict Patrick Seton, who goes to prison and cannot take Alice to Austria to murder her. Elsie Forrest, then, saves her friend's life and helps in ways that she would not have imagined—nor did Ronald Bridges.

The verdict against Patrick Seton is evidence of justice in the world. Further, it is described by both Seton and Alice as a "test of God." Alice's reaction is important: "I don't believe in God," she says, but she clutches her stomach. Thus Muriel Spark reminds us of the unborn child, whose material presence has been felt. *The Bachelors* concludes with a statement that, before the baby was born, Alice married Matthew Finch, Ronald's Catholic friend. Worried about original sin, obsessed by sex, and concerned with family duty, Matthew finds her pregnancy attractive. His marriage to her means, of course, that he is no longer a bachelor.

Ronald Bridges, Spark's mouthpiece in the novel, remains one of the bachelors of London, a city with "thirty-eight thousand and five hundred streets, and seventeen point one bachelors to a street." He is an unusual bachelor, the epileptic who, like the artist, has a special vision that brings moral responsibility. Ronald accepts this by his insistence upon the truth, even when it is embarrassing and painful. He is sometimes depressed, but he persists in a belief in goodness and finds it through charity. In *The Bachelors*, there is thus a sense of amplitude, and the next novel is a further investigation of this quality.

The Girls of Slender Means

Sharp delineation of a group of young women who
are closely associated in an institution, related *The
Girls of Slender Means* to Spark's immediately
preceding novel, *The Prime of Miss Jean Brodie*.
However, its connections with *The Ballad of Peckham
Rye* and *The Bachelors* were more significant: the
scene is again London, and the central character a
young man. The doubling aspect of Dougal Douglas is
reiterated in this hero's early ambivalences. These are
finally replaced by a pervasive Roman Catholicism, as
in Ronald Bridges's life, but here it is extended to martyrdom.

The interest in *The Girls of Slender Means* is,
however, different; here Spark considered how
someone acquires religious conviction. Nicholas
Farrington's conversion is more than a philosophical
conviction; he becomes a missionary in Haiti. Thus
belief is translated into community effort. Spark made
a bold statement about how Divine Grace operates,
setting apart those who receive it.

A Reuters news report of Nicholas's martyrdom is
the catalyst for the narrative. Jane Wright, now a
woman columnist in London, knew him "long ago in
1945," when first he visited the May of Teck Club as
her guest. She telephones their mutual acquaintances,
seeking information that might explain something
about the man who preached against local superstitions in Haiti and was killed in a deserted spot when
everyone had gone to market on a day in 1960. Jane
wants to write a big article, but she also would like to
understand the interesting story. Not everyone knows
a martyr. But all those she calls remember little about
Nicholas and are indifferent. This is ironic, since his
experiences during the brief months that he was
associated with "the girls of slender means" at the May
of Teck Club set the direction of his life. The novel

describes that "long ago time" only after establishing
the perspective of Nicholas's martyrdom, and Jane's
telephone conversations are interlaced throughout the
narrative.

The story is simply outlined. Nicholas is very
friendly with the inhabitants of a wartime hostel, especially the youngest group who live on the top floor.
He is introduced by Jane and becomes particularly
aware of Johanna Childe, a rector's daughter whose
elocution practice provides a constant gloss on the action, through poetry aptly chosen to reinforce the
novel's theme. However, Nicholas loves the beautiful
and elegant Selina. The climax comes with the
detonation of an unexploded bomb that has lain un-
detected in the garden. In the resultant fire Johanna is
killed, and Selina's cold selfishness is recognized by
Nicholas. He changes from an indulgent and uncertain
would-be utopian visionary to a religious missionary
who abandons all to follow Christ. As poet, he moves
from youthful confidence to disillusionment, but as a
missionary, he maintains belief and human contact.

The main action of *The Girls of Slender Means* takes
place in 1945, during the long summer between VE
Day and VJ Day, between the end of the Second
World War in Europe and its final conclusion in the
Far East. Between May and August people begin to
think of possibilities that did not occur when actions
were determined by the war. Spark continues her
evocative creation of time and place by concentrating
her attention on a small community whose members
are individually realized and representative but who
also develop symbolically. Again there is a transfiguration of the commonplace; a very serious theme is
presented lightly and wittily through deft charac-
terization, memorable incident, and distinctive
dialogue.

The May of Teck Club is situated in Kensington
near the Albert Memorial. An Edwardian foundation,

the club exists for "the Pecuniary Convenience and Social Protection of Ladies of Slender Means below the age of Thirty Years, who are obliged to reside apart from their families in order to follow on Occupation in London." There are forty-odd women in residence, but the novel focuses on three. Compared to others, the young women who live in the hostel are "more delightful, more ingenious, more movingly lovely, and, as it might happen, more savage." Such contrasts and heightened responses provoke complex evaluations.

Nicholas Farrington is fascinated. Thirty-three years old when he is brought to the club for dinner, he is a son of a good English family and Cambridge educated. Nicholas is a poet and an anarchist. He has been undecided about many things—where to live, sexual preferences, religion, suicide, pacificism. Through an aesthetic and ethical conception of the May of Teck Club, he finds an embodiment of his ideal. He envisions human governance without institutions, "ruled by the corporate will of men's hearts alone." Because of this "lovely, frozen image," he is somewhat in love with all of the girls of slender means, but he sleeps with Selina Redwood, who is the most beautiful and extremely slim, but also very self-centered and self-indulgent.

Selina's "austere and economically furnished" body inspires Nicholas, who wants her "to be an ideal society personified amongst her bones." His vision of Selina as a symbol of poverty is, however, a far cry from the reality of the calculating self-seeker who uses people and occasions unscrupulously. Selina has taken a Poise Course, and twice each day recites an exercise, a kind of sacred text to keep her self-confident: "Poise is perfect balance, an equanimity of body and mind, complete composure whatever the social scene." So completely is Selina controlled by this dictum that she performs an act of savagery that provides Nicholas with a moment of revelation.

The surface poise of the May of Teck Club, like the immediate ease of any circumstance, masks latent danger and destruction. Greggie, an older member of the Club, insists there is an unexploded bomb in the garden, an analogue to the atomic bomb that is dropped on Hiroshima. Greggie's apprehension becomes a reality that provides the climax of the action. A fire results from the explosion, and many are trapped in the building. Because Selina is so slender, she easily escapes through the bathroom window to the roof, a route she has often used to join Nicholas, who came from the adjacent building to enjoy making love to her. While other girls are waiting to be rescued, Selina calmly reenters the building to save a treasured Schiaparelli dress. Her attention is entirely upon this lovely taffeta evening garment, an image of her social seeking, a showy sign of her superficial way of life. It is owned by Anne Baberton but worn by all the girls who are slender, so that it provides a kind of communal focus. Selina cares for the sign and has no concern for those whose lives are endangered.

This is the crucial moment for Nicholas; he is forced "involuntarily to make an entirely unaccustomed gesture, the signing of the cross upon himself." Thus Spark makes the theological point that Divine Grace comes "involuntarily," not by seeking. Nicholas was, of course, in a state of readiness. His unpublished manuscript is called *The Sabbath Notebooks*, and a note explains that "a vision of evil may be as effective to conversion as a vision of good." Selina's callous behavior clarifies Nicholas's uncertainties. The course of his life is changed, for an apparently trival event has great significance. When Selina asks him whether they are safe out on the rooftop, Nicholas replies, "Nowhere's safe." He perceives that the material world cannot offer perfection, and thus he seeks something beyond it. He finally becomes decisive when he chooses the way of the spirit.

Nicholas's decision is reinforced on the night of VJ Day when, in the midst of exuberant public celebrations, he witnesses another act of savagery. He alone sees a seaman stab a woman; amid the tumultuous crowd, cries are not heard, and he is swept away. A little later he finds himself next to the murderer and puts into his pocket a letter that Jane has forged. Nicholas planned to use the letter to impress his potential publisher, Huy Throvis-Mew, whose private name is George Johnson. This is a gesture, a sign that Nicholas is renouncing the pursuit of fame as an artist. Indeed he simply gives *The Sabbath Notebooks* to Rudi Bittesch, a Rumanian who buys Jane's letters from famous authors. As a Christian missionary, Nicholas brings the Word in another way, and he dies far away from the girls of slender means.

The May of Teck Club is a microscosm, and Spark's title suggests the limitations of its inhabitants: the girls are poor in the austerity of the war, some are physically thin, and all lack moral resources. A partial exception to the last is Johanna Childe, whose name suggests innocence and closeness to Christ. Her life differs from those of the other inhabitants of the club, for she makes moral value judgments. Remaining loyal to her first love—an absolute commitment to the idea that there can be only one love as in marriage—and to a principle of self-denial, she does not allow herself a second suitor after her first love was not reciprocated. Nobly intentioned, Johanna yet remains an anomaly, removed from human experience but still not apart. Fair and healthy, Johanna is a person of intense feeling, but this is sublimated through poetry, which "excited and possessed her."

Spark uses the elocution selections to parallel the narrative action; they serve as chorus. For example,

Johanna recites lines from Gerard Manley Hopkins's *The Wreck of the Deutschland*, and her death resembles that of the nuns in the poem. The person of integrity dies violently, and the only explanation is that God teaches through fear. Certainly this is Nicholas's response, and Johanna has a sense of Hell. Johanna's self-abnegation is a foil to Selina's self-absorption. She is aware of a reality beyond this world, but this is not like the mad imaginings of a lover, recounted by another club member Pauline Fox. Johanna's "disinterestedness" shows in the recitation of poetry and choice of lines "the slightest bit melancholy on the religious side." Beautiful language and high sentiment resound and provide a contrast to the trivial and mundane, the solipsism that limits most people.

Muriel Spark's *The Girls of Slender Means* presents a vision of Divine Grace, which never comes unbidden but is so strongly felt that anything else is diminished. Not everyone recognizes the manifestation of Grace; Nicholas is only barely remembered when Jane Wright makes her telephone calls, and the death of Johanna is hardly recalled. No one—except the reader, for whom Spark, with two time sequences, has provided a detached perspective—is even clear about what happened. So how can they possibly understand why it happened? Nicholas tapes Johanna's recital of her favorite Hopkins's poem, and the lines spoken are: "Thou mastering me/ God! . . . Thou hast bound bones and veins in me, fastened me flesh,/ And after it almost unmade. . . . " Preceded by a conversation about sex and the Beatific Vision—earthly and heavenly ecstasy—these lines describe the awareness that comes with "growing in grace" and lets one "take everything in stride."

With such awareness, Johanna responds calmly to the crisis of the fire and to the panic. She recites the day's liturgy (thus soothing the others) and waits until everyone else is out before starting herself. She offers herself up to the Lord in an episode that prefigures Nicholas's martyrdom in Haiti. The tape of Johanna's recital is accidentally erased, both Johanna and Nicholas die violently, but the novel preserves their memories through its vision and poetry. Martydrom is rather out of fashion in modern times, and Spark's creation of Christian saints in *The Girls of Slender Means* was unusual, an extraordinary apotheosis that extended beyond her familiar commonplaces. In her next novel, she returned to the pilgrim way more familiar in this life.

7

The Pilgrim Way

The Mandelbaum Gate

The Mandelbaum Gate, in many ways Muriel Spark's most ambitious work, is memorable for a variety of reasons. First, its larger scope makes possible more detailed exposition of plot and delineation of setting and character. In an interview at the time of its publication, Spark explained that it had taken her two years to write *The Mandelbaum Gate*, while *The Prime of Miss Jean Brodie* took her eight weeks. She spent two months in Israel, and as a result it is "much more concrete and solidly rooted in a very detailed setting"[1] in which Spark had not previously lived.

Second, though it describes outrageous situations and hilarious and satirical moments, *The Mandelbaum Gate* is Spark's most traditional novel. Its straightforward characterizations closely resemble those found in conventional fiction because they present fuller, rounder figures than are seen in most of Spark's work. Time and place are precisely indicated, and incidents that are bizarre and nothing else occur less often in *The Mandelbaum Gate* than in, for example, *The Ballad of Peckham Rye* or *Not to Disturb*. Finally, many biographical details are easily identifiable in the book, making it personal in ways that Spark's other novels are not. One result of these innovations in the author's approach is to give *The Man-delbaum Gate* a documentary quality; another is a religious sense that is infrequently articulated in the modern world where reality is usually defined as nothing more than surface appearance.

The precise setting is Jerusalem in August of 1961, the first year of the Eichmann trial. This long-sought Nazi and his horrendous crimes against the Jews captured worldwide attention; however, Spark sees the trial as but a passing detail in the complex history of Jerusalem. By treating the Eichmann case only incidentally, she suggests both the ordinariness of evil and the diminishing importance of any event when it is placed in the perspective of time. Jerusalem appears on medieval maps as the center of the temporal world; modern knowledge of geography discredits this notion, but the city's significance as a focus for Judaism, Christianity, and Islam persists. Jerusalem is an anticipation of the heavenly or celestial city: "Jerusalem, my happy home,/ When shall I come to thee?" as an old text puts it. This symbolic identity is intensely important in *The Mandelbaum Gate*, which to a greater extent than any of Spark's other novels interweaves reality and allegory.

The Holy Land is a locus for intrigue, and Spark exploits the exotic quality of mixed cultures and dangerous differences between Arab and Jew while she tells an exciting and suspenseful story. By including political topicality in the personal story of her characters, she creates the quality of a thriller. There is real peril in the antipathy between Arab and Jew, an antipathy that is embodied in the divided city. The separation of the two parts of Jersualem is marked by the Mandelbaum Gate, "hardly a gate at all, but a piece of street between Jerusalem and Jerusalem, flanked by two huts, and called by that name because a house at the other end once belonged to a Mr. Mandelbaum." The title of the book, then, is a symbol for

both the reality and the illusion of the division between Arab and Jew. The action amplifies this duality
through secret movements, disguises, smuggling, and
spying, and points up the irony of it by focusing on
tourism and pilgrimages to religious sites on both sides
of the dividing line.

At the center of the novel is Barbara Vaughan, a
thirty-seven-year-old teacher of English, a spinster
who looks severe and seems to have no feelings,
definitely "the safe type." The chapter title "Barbara
Vaughan's Identity" states a major theme. The heroine
is very sure of who she is, but she recognizes that "her
self-image was at variance with the image she presented to the world." Barbara's appearance shows years
of cautious living, but that pattern has changed
markedly with her love for archaeologist Harry Clegg.

Although Barbara and Harry enjoyed a passionate
love affair during the previous summer, they have not
married. Harry is divorced, but they are hoping for an
annulment that will allow them to marry in the
Roman Catholic Church. Indeed, while Barbara is on
her pilgrimage to the Holy Land, Harry is in Rome to
present his case to the Congregation of the Rota in the
hope that his first marriage will be judged not valid.
Even though Barbara decided that she will marry
Harry regardless of the outcome of his case, she
worries. She knows that marriage outside the Church
would be difficult, since only within the Church can
she have peace of mind. Thus she doubts her courage
in continuing her resolve.

Religion is central to Barbara's existence. Her heritage is a complex one. With a Jewish mother and a
Christian father, she experienced an upbringing that
included no formal religion. Her conversion to Roman
Catholicism was thus a crucial way of defining herself.
Her decision to convert, based on intellectual choice
rather than feeling, was made only after long consideration. As is apparent to all, Barbara Vaughan's

religion is a matter of conviction, "something absolutely undisplaceable in her nature."[2]

The reserved and diffident Barbara is more intense
than she appears. Just as no one suspects her sexual
liaison, so few recognize that one major attraction to
the Roman Catholic Church for her is not its firm and
clear orthodoxy but rather "its recognition of the
helpless complexity of motives that prompted an action, and its consequent emphasis on actual words,
thoughts and deeds; there was seldom one motive in
the grown person; the main thing was that motives
should harmonize."

Thus Barbara Vaughan goes on her pilgrimage to
Jerusalem with mixed motives. She is waiting for news
about the annulment, although she has already made
up her mind to marry Harry. She wants to visit the key
sites in the Holy Land, but she also wants to escape
from her life in England, particularly the exclusive
personal claims and pressures exerted by Ricky (Miss
Rickward), the headmistress of her school and a longtime personal friend. Though Barbara's appearance is
retiring, she is a passionate woman, committed in
many ways, and she has not yet resolved many conflicts in her attitudes and life.

Jerusalem is an appropriate place for Barbara to be.
She is keenly aware of its historical and religious
significance, but she also recognizes that current
inhabitants, like those before them, exploit this and
even make fraudulent assertions about sites to en-
courage pilgrims and tourists. Because a news item
identifies Barbara as the child of a Jewish mother, she
would be prudent not to enter Jordan. Nevertheless,
she "must have the whole pilgrimage." She visits both
Israel and Jordan because she wants to experience all
parts of her heritage. Although she is a Roman
Catholic, Barbara has not cut herself off from her
Jewish family. Indeed she firmly believes in the harmony of the Old and New Testaments. Her attitude

toward Scripture is symptomatic; she insists on their importance to her friend Saul Ephraim but then, in English fashion, softens the assertion with a timid laugh. As someone with great sympathy for Jews, she could be expected to resent Arabs. But Barbara finds Abdul and Suzi Ramdez appealing, perhaps because they also have ambivalent attitudes toward the complex claims of Jerusalem. Their extraordinary father, Joe Ramdez, she accepts as an endearing cheat. In short, Barbara recognizes the limitations of simple labeling. Knowing herself to be a composite of qualities that are superficially contradictory, she seeks resolution through charitable response rather than simplistic judgment.

How to cope with such divisions is a major theme in *The Mandelbaum Gate*, and the basis is laid for this question in the opening chapter, which introduces Freddy Hamilton and concludes with his meeting Barbara. An English career diplomat, Freddy, who is a favorite at dinner and cocktail parties, charms his hostesses with poetic thank-yous but resists the temptation of personal involvements. Having diplomatic immunity, he crosses easily from Jordan to Israel, and he prefers noncommittal personal behavior that allows a similar ease of human traffic. Freddy is an unlikely romantic hero, but he briefly assumes this role in the central action of *The Mandelbaum Gate*. With known Jewish ancestry, Barbara imprudently enters Jordan. Freddy recognizes that she is in danger and decides to become a knight champion to rescue her. Because Barbara develops scarlet fever, she cannot leave immediately and, through several coincidences, is placed in a house used by an espionage ring that has eluded the British foreign service but is finally uncovered by the dynamic Freddy. With his new sense of self, Freddy also makes love to Suzi. This dramatic shift in Freddy's attitudes and behavior is an affirmation of human potential for active commitment, even in

one who is cautiously "nice" and known to be "sweet."
Freddy is very like Barbara was before she fell in love
with Harry Clegg. They share a comfortable and
decorous Englishness, but soon after they meet at the
hotel the limitations of Freddy's temperate charm,
with its concomitant insensitivity, become clear to an
agitated Barbara. Recognizing the differences between the two of them, she quotes a passage from the
Apocalypse:

I know of thy doings, and find thee neither cold nor hot,
cold or hot, I would thou wert one or the other. Being what
thou art, lukewarm, neither cold nor hot, thou wilt make me
vomit thee out of my mouth.

Barbara has already passed from lukewarm to hot,
and that transition is eventually mirrored in Freddy
when he quotes the same passage to the Cartwrights,
his English friends in Jordan. Freddy's later loss of
memory of that Saturday night to Tuesday afternoon
when he is engaged in this uncharacteristic behavior is
a mark of his limitation, his uneasiness with the active
role. In retrospect, however, he thinks that the effect
of the experience was "to transfigure his life, without
any disastrous change in the appearance of things."
The religious implication of his words is reinforced by
Spark's reference to Freddy's recalling events "like a
cloud of unknowing." The mystic term, best known in
the title of a fourteenth-century English book of contemplation, signifies man's inability to understand and
to describe, even while knowing, because the truths
about God are so overwhelming that they are known
only through love.[3]

Freddy, of course, is not a religious person; he admits that the Apocalypse is "beyond him." His
pilgrimage of life is not like Barbara's, for he lacks the
love needed to undertake positive, active seeking.
Early in the novel Barbara expresses belief in the
Transfiguration of Jesus, but rationally admits that the
exact site is open to question, though the basilica on

Mount Tabor is the spot with strongest claims. Freddy
has no such faith. Still, he is a decent man who occasionally can be stirred from the characteristic inertia
he disguises with good manners and evasiveness, and
for a brief time he forswears personal convenience and
safety to help Barbara. Such active involvement makes
him feel free, giving him an unexpected release from
his more characteristic impersonality. The result of the
experience is similar to that of Barbara's love for
Harry. The individual is no longer controlled by the
older constraints of a narrow life and becomes both a
more distinctive person and a part of the larger being
that is not limited to individuals.

Nevertheless, Barbara's complexity of experience
and persistent efforts to revise her habits of mind so
that she can cope with this complexity keep her
"transfiguration" distinct from Freddy's. His is a
momentary expansion and a memory of it afterward;
hers is an enlarged and also an evolving perception. In
addition to "honest, analytical intelligence" and
fidelity to the observable, Barbara possesses "the
beautiful and dangerous gift of faith, which by
definition of the Scriptures, is the sum of things hoped
for and the evidence of things unseen." This sense of
transcendence makes all the difference. Like others,
Barbara has defined herself as part of certain
groups—Gentile, Jew, spinster, teacher, Catholic.
However, she is always alert to similarities, for example, those that exist between the experiences of the Sufi
woman mystic of the eighth century and Christian
mystics. Jerusalem reflects both the human urge for
group membership and the divisiveness and conflict
that are the consequences of such sentiments. The
separated sections of the city, the tension among the
different peoples, the paranoia and singleminded obsessiveness, indicate that reconciliation, like that
realized by Barbara Vaughan, is indeed rare.

Spark's use of the Eichmann trial as a counterpoint

underscores the horrors of divisions that, as in this extreme manifestation, mean an attempt to exterminate a species. In *The Prime of Miss Jean Brodie*, Spark explored fascism; *The Mandelbaum Gate* restates her aversion to dominating groups and the leaders who exploit them. In the relatively innocuous remarks of casual conversation and social commerce that are noted in the book, bias appears in racial, religious, political, and class intolerance. Anyone who, like Freddy, is completely identified with a single group, is especially vulnerable to solipsism. He is not given to love, which is "never a sin and thus not to be repented." Those of mixed origins and several allegiances, like Barbara or the Ramdez family, are more likely to be detached and less likely to be complacent, and thus they often respond with humorous tolerance.

Barbara's version of Catholicism, which embraces the larger essentials but avoids the smaller restrictions, is a vivid illustration of her healthy skepticism. Barbara perceives both the oneness of being and the interrelatedness of various parts of her experience, and she expresses this vision in a conversation with Suzi Ramdez. In a friendly way, the young Arab woman questions the sincerity of the English woman's religious devotions because Barbara jokes about love affairs. Barbara notes:

> Well, either religious faith penetrates everything in life or it doesn't. There are some experiences that seem to make nonsense of all separations of sacred from profane—they seem childish. Either the whole of life is united under God or everything falls apart. Sex is child's play in the argument.

This simple statement argues a resolution of the duality of man's physical and spiritual, instinctual and rational, natures. Barbara's comment is an open statement of an earlier meditation on sex in Spark's narrative:

> Sex is child's play. Jesus Christ was very sophisticated on

the subject of sex. And didn't harp on it. Why is it so predominant and serious for us? There are more serious things in the world. And if sex is not child's play, in any case it is worthless. For she was thinking of her own recent experiences of sex, which were the only experiences she knew worth thinking about. It was child's play, unselfconscious and so full of fun and therefore of peace that she had not bothered to analyse or define it. And, she thought, we have invented guilt to take our minds off the real thing.

These two passages are among the most forthright of all Spark's statements about morality in the modern world. They point up the absurdity of the simplistic reduction of man's moral nature to a mere concern about his sexual behavior. The reference to Christ suggests the discrepancy between the Gospels and subsequent "Christian" practices. Spark's argument asserts the significance of sex as play, as a part of the cosmic game, and affirms that it is simple and personal and not a subject for public discussion. Also implied is the necessity for devoting greater attention to serious things, those issues that are central to the novel—class snobbery, religious bigotry, political fanaticism, solipsism. These truly serious issues require moral discernment, a thoughtful understanding and concomitant changes of attitudes by responsible individuals, however indifferent the world may be to them.

The crucial moment of Barbara Vaughan's decision that she complete her pilgrimage to the Holy Land comes when she attends the Eichmann trial. She does not go during the sensational stories of the death camps but while the plodding accounts of details, timetables and transport problems, are read, "the dull phase [that] was in reality the heart of the trial." Eichmann "was not answering for himself or his own life at all, but for an imperative deity named Bureau IV-B-4, of whom he was High Priest." The system in which the Nazi worshipped was false; his defense that his actions were selfless is a consummate horror, an utter distortion, the more terrifying because it is given as a substitute for a kind of religion. Responding to the inhumanity of Eichmann's case, Barbara recognizes, without awareness of "any disruption in logic of personal decisions," that she will complete her pilgrimage in Jordan in spite of the risks. She refuses to submit to a system of division that violates her integrity, of which her Jewish heritage is a part. In a discussion of new French writers Barbara identifies the modern condition—"repetition, boredom, despair, going nowhere for nothing, all of which conditions are enclosed in a tight, unbreakable statement of the times at hand."[4]

Barbara refuses to accept this common modern viewpoint and aligns herself with another ethos. Heeding the injunction of the Apocalypse, she is not lukewarm. She takes risks; her life's business is seeking, not simply enduring. Further, she admits there are elements that are unpredictable and unexplainable and, so admitting, she surrenders to that which is beyond her. Barbara is independent, but she also needs the help of others when she becomes ill in Jordan. Freddy helps her to escape from the convent in Jordan; Ruth Gardnor cares for her as she is recovering from scarlet fever; Abdul conducts her illegal return to Israel. And Barbara believes that none of this goes wrong because it is all in God's providence.

She not only accepts the many different things that happen to her, she also calmly "gloats" and is even wryly amused. When Ruth Gardnor is frightened because she believes Barbara is part of an Arab nationalist spy organization that communicates with Cairo, Barbara notes that she "must be a hell of an important agent." It is all "a great experience," and her return to safety is highly comic. Barbara crosses back into Israel dressed as a nun; she is accompanied by Abdul, who is disguised as a tonsured Franciscan, unlikely though this is for an Arab. Once in Jerusalem she runs along the narrow streets where the orthodox

Jews live, and Abdul runs after—an astonishing sight to all the passers-by. This is an extraordinary end to Barbara's pilgrimage, resonating with the playful laughter that comes from recognition of how limited is human understanding of what is actually happening. What appears is not what is: Barbara and Abdul are not members of religious communities, and they have not lost their wits; they—Catholic, Jew, Arab—are together and in harmony, and they are safe again.

Perhaps because of its large scale, Spark made the structure of *The Mandelbaum Gate* obvious: it is divided into two parts with titled chapters.[5] The second part consists of only one long chapter, and its title "The Passionate Pilgrims" succinctly states the novel's theme. The basic metaphor of the book, the pilgrimage of life, has its origins in Scripture, and the idea dominated Christian thought after the twelfth century. Barbara's story evolves as an actual physical trip to the Holy Land to visit sacred places and also as the seeking that characterizes the full expression of an individual life.

The latter, as Barbara notes, can be all-inclusive: "Everything's a subject for a Christian pilgrimage if you widen the scope enough." Although she began her trip with definite objectives, she finds that her experiences as a pilgrim are quite different from what she originally intended. However, such discrepancies between human expectation and experience are made acceptable through a recognition that "With God, everything is possible." Thus, when Barbara is in greatest physical danger—ill, alone, a half-Jew in Jordan—she takes "one of her religious turns, and was truly given to the love of God, and all things were possible." Similarly, Freddy finds, when he embarks upon his elaborate rescue plans, that "all was perfectly possible, or as good as done, and he walked in that dispensation of mind in which impossible works are in fact accomplished and mountains moved." Human beings are, then, capable of much more than they can imagine for themselves; they are often less in control than they assume.

Finally, it is not the careful efforts of Barbara and Harry to have his marriage annulled that resolve the dilemma. A vindictive Ricky provides a copy of a baptismal certificate for Harry (a false document) to prove that he is a Roman Catholic. Her intention is to prevent Barbara's marriage to him, but she unwittingly provides evidence that, from a Catholic point of view, his first marriage was invalid. Catholics can only be married by Catholic priests and Harry's first marriage was not a Catholic one, so there is no longer an obstacle to his marrying Barbara, since in the eyes of the Church he has never been married. Barbara sees this as "marvelous." A priest at the hotel affirms that Barbara and Harry will be able to have a valid marriage. He is Father Colin Ballantyne, whose sermon she had heard and whose party she had accompanied on her return through the Mandelbaum Gate. Father Colin thinks he recognizes her but is puzzled; he is "left with the mystery." Here Spark's choice of words suggests both thriller and theology. Father Colin's reappearance in the novel suggests both coincidence and providence. The marvel, the mystery, signify how paltry are man's understanding and power. This idea is restated in the concluding paragraph that centers on Freddy, rather than the central character of the novel, who walks around the places of history and reenters Jerusalem through the Mandelbaum Gate, a nondescript spot that is named for someone who is otherwise unremembered.

The play of history is this novel denotes much more than the significance of an ancient site crucial to three of the world's great religions and traditionally a meeting place of East and West. It leads to thoughts of passing time, and the length of the novel reinforces this sense of flow. The dramatic events of Barbara's pilgrimage, and the smaller pilgrimages of others, are set against a larger story of history, itself only temporary and dimly suggesting the possibilities of a celestial Jerusalem. Barbara Vaughan is Muriel Spark's most completely realized character, a sympathetic and extraordinarily poised individual. Without utterly abandoning her satirist's eye and wickedly witty language, the novelist is gentler and wooingly persuasive in *The Mandelbaum Gate*. On its publication, many reviewers found the novel disappointing, and subsequently it has not been greatly praised. Perhaps its idealism and faith were too much at variance with the thinking and lifestyles of the 1960s. At any rate, Spark's next novel began a very different phase.

8

The Darkening Vision

The Public Image

While *The Mandelbaum Gate* is pervaded with a sense of deep spiritual strength, *The Public Image* deals with pretense. Barbara Vaughan's unprepossessing appearance conceals extraordinary personal resources, but Annabel Christopher's dazzling image hides basic personal limitations. Spark's characteristic heroine—sensitive, intelligent, thoughtful, religious, articulate—is replaced in *The Public Image* by a woman who lacks these qualities. The new heroine is, in fact, "stupid," a mere "shell," a surface below which there is little. Nevertheless, Annabel finally experiences a moral awakening and decides to stand apart from the trivial and corrupt. Thus the novel is related to Spark's earlier fiction, which expresses a gradual increasing faith in the human possibility of God's creation. However, *The Public Image* also signaled a darkening phase in Spark's work, when her fiction mirrors the uncertainty, confusion, infidelity, and violence that are ordinary characteristics of contemporary society. The story of *The Public Image* uses materials familiar in film magazines and newspapers, a frequent source of Spark's ideas.[1] The setting was Rome, the place of *la dolce vita*—international celebrities, wealth, fleeting fame, decadence.[2]

Annabel Christopher's public image is the English Lady-Tiger of the cinema, and she works hard to sustain this role, which was created by the director Luigi Leopardi. Without the illusions of the camera, she looks like what she is—a puny English girl from Wakefield. On the screen she expresses, largely because the director transforms her eyes, well-bred sexuality. The artist as novelist in Spark's early fiction is here replaced by the cinema director, who defines life as "all the achievement of an effect." *The Public Image* explores illusion and reality. A careful publicity campaign reinforces the Lady-Tiger image by showing the same characteristics that Annabel presents on the screen in her personal life, in her marriage to the writer Frederick Christopher.

At age thirty-two Annabel is very successful, but she is terribly limited. While the actress accepts that she need not be clever and merely has to exist in front of the cameras, her writer husband is offended by "shallowness." Frederick sees this in their personal lives and in the lives of movie celebrities in Rome. He expresses his fury finally in absolute ways: he commits suicide and provides evidence that a blackmailer can use against Annabel.

Fredrick's anger and his relentless intention to destroy "the public image" keep him from adequate recognition of Annabel's latent strength. This both comes from and is demonstrated by her love for their baby, whom she shelters from publicity and whose innocence she defends. Thus Annabel is able to resist the threat of blackmail, and even to destroy the public image that she has exploited and, at the end of the novel, she looks forward to a truer life.

Resenting his wife's role-playing, Frederick became obsessed with the enormity of her deception. His first defense was to cultivate his own image as the serious writer and would-be actor who is somehow too good for "the film kind of thing." Thus he chooses to make his personal life an artifice, of which the climax is his carefully planned and executed suicide. He sets out to destroy the public image by showing Annabel as an unfaithful wife, negligent mother, and indulger in orgies. Frederick builds his case by writing a series of notes and by arranging that a dissolute group appears at their flat for a party at the precise time that he throws himself from the scaffolding at the site where the martyrdom of St. Paul took place. As the artist plays God, manipulating characters and shaping lives, he shows himself to be an utter personal failure. But Frederick is still dangerous because suicide is a criminal act, something that Annabel cannot afford to be associated with.

When the suicide notes are produced by Frederick's old friend Billy O'Brien, a known blackmailer, Annabel instantly recognizes the professional finesse of her enemy. She tries to defend herself against false charges and guilty appearances. She argues that Frederick has only an idea, not the reality of her when he asserts: "You are a beautiful shell, like something washed up on the sea-shore, a collector's item, perfectly formed, a pearly shell—but empty, devoid of the life it once held." The poet-maker eloquently indulges his fancy, creating his own personae. The real Annabel is neither the public image of cinematic (and publicity) creation nor the private image of Frederick's resentment. She has passively accepted her role as Lady-Tiger with the expectation of discarding it as her career evolves. She, of course, plays a part for Frederick, being judicious, amusing, and uncritical. Further, she acts—the precisely staged press conference, the visit to the hospital, planting a defense —to preserve the Lady-Tiger image because she believes it a valid one. This role has given her confidence and competence she had not possessed. These traits also appear offscreen; she has been efficient in arranging for the decoration of the flat in Rome.

Annabel is humble, faintly surprised by her success in films. She typically does not try to force her will on others. Even Frederick is a willing actor in the script his wife enacts, but Annabel knows almost nothing about her husband or his activities just before his death. The personal cost to Frederick of her image never occurs to Annabel, who thus fails as a human being. However, with all her bland indifference, she retains a deep, instinctual knowledge of the limitations of the public image. The source of this awareness is her baby, who is identified with reality, and Annabel jealously separates him from the rest of her life. Several exquisite scenes show her caring for little Carl; poised and serene, she gains strength from his warm presence. Annabel's tragic misfortune lies in fragmentation, in her inability to fuse her public and private lives into a harmonious oneness.

On balance, however, she is more in touch with reality than her far too rational, intellectual, deliberate husband. Muriel Spark repeatedly voices distrust of such personalities, particularly when they are self-conscious. Annabel refuses to mortgage her freedom and her baby's by paying a blackmailer to suppress the suicide notes; she wants "to be free like her baby." Intuitively, not intellectually, she makes the right moral choice. Her new anonymity, bold evidence that she is no longer the captive of the public image, is not disturbing. At Rome airport, when she is leaving behind her old life as a film star, Annabel neither wants to be recognized nor to meet an old friend from her past. Annabel lets the stewardess take her bags; the baby she wants to carry on the plane herself.

The final paragraph of *The Public Image*, which is as finely written as any in modern fiction, definitively describes the nature of Annabel Christopher:

Waiting for the order to board, she felt both free and un-free. The heavy weight of the bags was gone; she felt as if she

was still, curiously, pregnant with the baby, but not
pregnant in fact. She was pale as a shell. She did not wear
dark glasses. Nobody recognized her as she stood, having
moved the baby to rest on her hip, conscious of the baby in a
sense weightlessly and perpetually within her, as an empty
shell contains, by its very structure, the echo and harking
image of former and former seas.

As in a poem, Muriel Spark repeats the language and
imagery that have established Annabel as a lukewarm
person, one who is not passionate or bolstered by an
intelligent conviction of her identity. Frederick called
her a beautiful empty shell, and this description has a
validity. But though pale, Annabel does not conceal
who she is (no dark glasses); also she is going on with
her life. Not giving up, incidentally, is her definition
of forgiveness, rather than a formal blessing or
statement. The one sure reality of her life, the baby
and the permanent sense of pregnancy (of
possibilities), transforms the commonplace. The shell
is placed in the eternal universe, and it is meaningful.

This conclusion is precisely appropriate for the kind
of woman Muriel Spark created. Annabel Christopher
is one of the nominal successes of the modern world
and a romantic. Muriel Spark distrusted both the
romantic, who is self-indulgent, and the intellectual.
Only through the destruction of Annabel's public
image can she possibly gain an integrity.

Whether Annabel would have made the decision to
abandon her public image without Frederick's suicide
is a moot question. Muriel Spark's consistent view was
that ambiguity in human action is inevitable, so that
absolute moral judgment is difficult if not impossible.
Nowhere is lack of judgment more likely than in a
suicide, which always causes speculation. Frederick's
choice of a site symbolic in its association with martyrdom, and Annabel's calling him a "martyr" in comments to the Italian press, give rise to the possibility
that the husband sacrifices his own life to force his

wife into a recognition and rejection of the public image. But there is ample evidence in the novel that Frederick, who is a more intense version of Godfrey Colston in *Memento Mori*, is an egotistical and jealous man, embittered by his own failures as an artist, and envious of his wife's success. He could be motivated by enmity and a wish to destroy. Or perhaps he is goaded by the new reality Annabel finds in their child, a reality he can neither share nor dismiss. Frederick demands that there be more behind the lovely exterior, just as Nicholas did of Selina in *The Girls of Slender Means*, and he cannot find in Annabel the complex personality that he demands. Annabel is a film star, but she does not belong to the world of effects which Leopardi creates and directs. Away from the camera, she is ordinary, even plain. Spark identifies her as "the natural animal" in her instinctual love for her child. Such "stupidity" may be momentarily circumvented, but it cannot long survive in the modern world. The discrepancy between Annabel's fame and screen image and her provincial simplicity off-screen infuriates Frederick. Thus she precipitates disaster, though quite unintentionally. The Lady-Tiger has not lived well; there is a chance that Annabel will fare better. The next novel, however, does not offer such optimism, for delusions become chronic in a terrifying heroine.

The Driver's Seat

Of all Muriel Spark's novels, *The Driver's Seat* is the most painful and disturbing to read, her bleakest book. Calling it "a study, in a way, of self-destruction," Spark said, "I frightened myself by writing it. . . . I had to go into hospital to finish it."[3] Her own obsessiveness paralleled the novel's materials. *The Driver's Seat* is about mania, abnormality; Spark's characteristic religious material has been eliminated, and her typical humor lessened. The

novel, her first to be narrated exclusively in the present
tense, is very much a ruthless evocation of the un-
naturalness and horror of contemporary life. The title
suggests an image of our world, where the automobile
dominates. The principal character says she is
"terrified" of traffic, "afraid" because, "You never
know what crackpot's going to be at the wheel of
another car."

Lise is herself a "crackpot," and the novel relates
how she assumes the driver's seat, never swerving until
she has achieved her objective of having someone murder her. The setting is "indeterminately somewhere in
Europe, in the south—not necessarily Italy." Spark
gave only an external view of the protagonist and those
she meets, a suitable technique for a study of
derangement. The solipsism that was so often her interest is here magnified to insanity. In earlier novels
Spark introduced a single scene of evil; here there is a
single scene of good. Lise's potential as a human being
is shown by her responding to Mrs. Fiedke and accepting a view of herself as "kind." "'Why shouldn't
I be kind,' Lise says, smiling at her with a sudden
gentleness."

Nevertheless, Lise is usually neither reassured nor
reassuring; she is "unkind"—lacking in generosity and
violating humanity. Everything is twisted. The purpose of a holiday becomes not restoration but destruction; female victim pursues male murderer. The case is
one for lurid press coverage, and in addition to the
central action there are accounts of macrobiotic
theories, student demonstrations, Middle East sheiks,
and the unnatural material products that seem all the
contemporary world offers. Thus Spark enlarged her
vision of an abnormal protagonist, who becomes a
terrifying archetype, known only through the brief,
continuous hours of her driving.

Lise is a nondescript person. She does not have a sur-
name, she lives "in the North" of Europe, and her

home is "nowhere special." She speaks four lan-
guages—English, French, Italian, and Danish.

Lise is thin. Her height is about five-foot-six. Her hair is pale
brown, probably tinted, a very light streaked lock sweeping
from the middle of her hair-line to the top of her crown; her
hair is cut short at the sides and back, and is styled high. She
might be as young as twenty-nine or as old as thirty-six, but
hardly younger, hardly older.

She is Spark's least specifically designated and per-
sonalized heroine. Having lived through the expectations of youth and acquired nothing, she becomes
irrevocably destructive. This novel is a chilling in-
dictment of the modern world in which people are utterly dehumanized by a barrenness of experience,
existing ceaselessly in "lukewarm" conditions. Lise has
doggedly kept her dull job in an accountant's office
"continually, except for the months of illness, since she
was eighteen, that is to say, for sixteen years and some
months." She lives in a functional one-room flat in
which the furniture lacks singularity—the bed is a seat
with bookcases by day, the writing table extends for
dining, and so on. It is "meticulously neat"; "Lise
keeps her flat as clean-lined and clear to return to after
work as if it were uninhabited. The swaying tall pines
among the litter of cones on the forest floor have been
subdued into silence and into obedient bulks." Human
beings, of course, are not so neatly and easily subdued
as woods, and the novel details the horrors of failed
humanity.

Lise is a study in mistaken careful control. After
years of undistinguished inanity, she pursues an
aggressive, disastrous course. There is no meaning in
her life, for she is one of the lukewarm who fail to
"transform the commonplace." Without this transfiguration, the human being is a kind of madman, and
Lise is so described with almost clinical precision.[4]
With chilling relentlessness, Spark chronicles the last

hours in the life of such a creature. Lise violently takes "the driver's seat." She is not professionally an artist, a maker, but she assumes godlike power, by presuming to determine her death with meticulous detail. Such misguided egotism is consistently decried in Spark's moral world, where there is usually an explicit acceptance of something in the universe beyond mere human whim and will.

The full poverty of Lise's being is clear when old Mrs. Fiedke asks how she will know when she has found the man for whom she is searching:

"Will you feel a presence? Is that how you'll know?"
"Not really a presence," Lise says. "The lack of an absence, that's what it is. I know I'll find it. I keep on making mistakes, though. . . . Too much self-control, which arises from fear and timidity, that's what's wrong with them [men]. They're cowards, most of them."

There is no real sense of possibility, only less difficulty; not happiness, just a lessened emptiness. Significantly, Lise accuses herself in ascribing the present malaise to "too much self-control, which arises from fear and timidity." In fact, most of the people she meets are not noticeably controlled by fear and timidity; they show a basic crassness and, indeed, aggression—the latter provoked, perhaps, by Lise's curiously abstracted manner. Self-control as Lise practices it, is self-destroying. No human life can be so completely disciplined, compartmentalized, deliberately divorced from the varied emotions that are the commonplaces of existence. Lise's absolute rejection of sexuality, for example, is given the lie by her needing a sex maniac to murder her.

Lise reveals herself very explicitly with the admission that she makes mistakes, an idea that is repeated several times in the novel. In the opening scene she has a tantrum in a shop when the assistant explains that the dress she is planning to buy does not stain. Furious at the implication that she might make a mistake and thus need a stain-resisting fabric, Lise flings off the garment and shouts, "I won't be insulted!" Even a suggestion of human fallibility is intolerable to someone so strenuously precise about details that she provides both exact instructions and necessary implements to the man she has commanded to murder her. However, with all her determination, and attention to details, Lise cannot have absolute control. Her chosen murderer insists upon altering one part of the proscribed pattern. Even the person in "the driver's seat" must adapt to the actions and wishes of passersby. But this would seem to be an oversimplification of the problem. Lise's response to the idea of flawless behavior is coupled with her awareness of how little impact human action seems to have in her world. Her anxiety and indignation are clear when she is talking to Mrs. Fiedke and declares, "As if I would want a dress that doesn't show the stains!"

Lise is obsessed with her own apartness and loneliness. Thus, when she goes to the Metropole to meet Bill, the advocate of macrobiotics, she tersely tells him, "You know nothing whatsoever about me." When he asks if she feels hungry, she replies, "No, I feel lonely." Peering into the closed, darkened Pavilion, she starts to cry again and notes "the inconceivable sorrow of it . . . all that lovely grief." Deeply involved in her own loneliness, she is quite oblivious to Bill. Certainly he is neurotically absorbed in his own macrobiotic regimen (specifically its required daily orgasm), but he shows concern when she cries. Bill's near rape is the more extraordinary since it comes after Lise had escaped the would-be Latin lover Carlo, to whom she had also appeared available. Briskly declaring "I'm not interested in sex," she stole his car with a threat of charging him with attempted rape if he dared to call the police.

In short, Lise is quite insensible to others. Even though she says, in the single human scene, "One should always be kind," she moves relentlessly toward her death—lying, stealing, cheating all those she encounters. They are harshly viewed and exploited by a woman who also obviously thinks herself contemptible. This is shown not only by her singleminded seeking of death, but also by her individual fabrications of another persona. She chooses a dress and coat of clashing, lurid colors, accurately asserting that they are right for her. "Very natural colors," wildly discordant in forced juxtaposition, suggest Lise's misguided and ruthless assertiveness of control. She feigns the experience of a sophisticated traveler at the airport, even falsifying her voice to an "ingratiating little girl tone" to address the attendant and her fellow passengers. For Carlo, she is a widow, an intellectual, and staying at the Hilton. These fabrications reveal a longing for importance, for stature, like that which came to Annabel Christopher through her public image.

Lise meets a surprising number of people during her last hours and almost always encounters a lack of humanity. She seems to hurtle on without a brief kindness or sympathy from the sniggering shopgirls who resent her eccentricity (and sales resistance), the portress who ridicules her, the obtuse South African matron on the plane, the hippy, and those who resent hippies, the sickly English aristocrat, the Middle Eastern sheik. All these testify to the lukewarm numbness of the modern world; some become just part of the cumulative investigation of a horrible murder. Muriel Spark reveals their stultifying incompetence as persons, with rapier precision.

Determined efforts to be murdered may well be defined as mad, but to regard Lise as an aberration, an unusual perversion of humanity, is not possible. Spark's world in *The Driver's Seat* is filled with creatures whose mindlessness is just short of Lise's disaster. Ironically, the individuals who least wish to injure Lise are those whom she most harms. Richard tries repeatedly, desperately, to escape her, to refuse to do her bidding. He is, of course, "her type." This young man has spent the last six years in a clinic and the two previous ones in prison. Richard claims to be cured and has tried throughout the day to escape Lise, who instantly identified him as a "sex-maniac."

Inexorably Lise produces the implements she has collected all day. Richard says quietly that "a lot of women get killed," and Lise agrees but insists that "they want to be . . . they look for it." The murder is very quickly done, though Richard's sexual violation precedes rather than follows it, as Lise, the driver, had planned. Just as she could not completely control her destiny, so Richard, who had "planned everything to be different," was not his own master. The investigating police will have to recognize that Richard alone was not guilty but "by chance" driven by Lise. The last lines of the novel suggest how inadequate modern society is in its inhumanity. Richard runs from the scene of his crime:

He sees already the gleaming buttons of the policeman's uniforms, hears the cold and the confiding, the hot and the barking voices, sees already the holsters and epaulets and all those trappings devised to protect them from the indecent exposure of fear and pity, pity and fear.

Heartlessness and resulting despair were never more intense and chilling than in this darkest phase of Spark's career.

Not to Disturb

If *The Driver's Seat* was spare and economical, *Not to Disturb* showed even greater paring away to a highly stylized dialogue that eliminated everything superfluous. Indeed, one reviewer suggested that perhaps the title was Muriel Spark's way of asking to be left to "the privacy of her own thoughts and reflections," to which she had retired.[6] She, however, described her motive as provoking the reader, "to startle as well as to please."[5] This she accomplished by again producing the unexpected, adapting conventional forms in distinctive ways.

The mainspring of the narrative is murders, but the interest centers not on the principals, the aristocratic Klopstocks, but upon their servants, who do not interrupt the violence that they hear in the library because they plan to exploit it. The novel focuses on the servants, who rehearse and prepare for the media their versions of the soon-to-be-accomplished murders. This pro-servant interest is an extravagant shift away from the usual emphasis. The butler is conventionally crucial in the denouement of a mystery story; here he becomes the controlling figure throughout the narrative.

The action is presented with effects characteristic of both the Gothic tale and Jacobean tragedy. Thus passion and murder occur on a stormy night with frightening natural elements, mysterious sounds come from the attic, a mad man appears to be the heir, dreams are premonitory. All this occurs in Switzerland, a nation with a modern tradition that rests on neutrality and monetary security—signs of lukewarm evasiveness and self-interest. The paradox of murder and noninterference is a counterpoint to the servants' actions. Because they "do not disturb," they are neutral and will gain vast wealth through the exploitation of "scandal exclusives" given to favored journalists. Indeed, the lack of moral awareness in the media is an important theme.

Set in Geneva, in an isolated great house described as "like a Swiss hotel, which you may be sure it will become," the action occurs during a night of careful waiting for the murders and suicide of Baron and Baroness Klopstock and Victor Passerat, their personal secretary and lover. The three have gone into the library for their customary sexual games, but these have become earnest, and the competent and determined butler

is halted by the Baron's afterthought—"Lister, if anyone calls, we aren't on any account to be disturbed." The Baron looks at the ormolu and blue enamelled clock, and then at his own wristwatch. "We don't want to be disturbed by anyone whomsoever." Lister moves his lips and head compliantly and leaves.

Thus the "not to disturb" motif is introduced, and the phrase appears fifteen times in the novel. The culmination is Lister's comment to Prince Eugene, a neighbor who tries to hire the servants after the stresses of the night and the morning's discoveries: "At the moment, sir," says Lister, "we want to go to sleep and we don't want to be disturbed." Servants take over the master's role.

Muriel Spark again not only entertained with comedy, suspense, and terror, but also looked at the basic moral questions in human control, detachment, and responsibility. The Baron's "afterthought" is an order scrupulously carried out, since the script that the servants are using calls for the principals to destroy themselves so that the domestics can garner large profits from exploiting the events in the mass media. All recognize that "It's Lister who decides." He is thus a figure, like Lise, in "the driver's seat." Lister argues: "Our position of privilege is unparalleled in history. The career of the domestic service is the thing of the future." Repeatedly his control is emphasized, and he directs the other servants, who think him "wonderful," "terrific," "marvelous," and praise his "sense of timing." Similarly, Lister compares the Baron to the pope and royalty; all, in their theatricality, suggest a stage production that shows careful setting and lighting. Indeed, the opening lines of *Not to Disturb* lead to a reading of the novel in these terms, for Lister—who is perhaps Muriel Spark's most literate figure, if one counts his allusions to Shakespeare, Marvell, James, Dickens, the Bible, and so on—quotes Webster's *The Duchess of Malfi* to describe the Klopstocks. "Their life," says Lister, "a general mist of error. Their death, a hideous storm of terror." And midway in the night of waiting for the murders he observes, "There remain a good many things to be accomplished and still more chaos effectively to organize."

Lister combines insensitivity to feeling with opportunistic and efficient manipulation of circumstances to exploit human weakness to his own advantage. He early recognizes the liability of involvement:

"How like," says Lister, "the death wish is to the life-urge! How urgently does an overwhelming obsession with life lead to suicide! Really, it's best to be half-awake and half-aware. That is the happiest stage."

The echo of the Book of the Apocalypse[7] is unmistakeable, but unlike Bosola in Webster's play, Lister does not modify his manipulative career. He will go on arranging details, and there seems no one to offset him. Indeed, he is encouraged, since so much advantage comes from his management. The clergyman, police, visiting aristocracy, journalists, all succumb to his efficiency that can survive even an error. Actually he turns his one miscalculation to advantage by altering the script to have pregnant Heloise marry the mad heir Gustav Anthony Klopstock, "him in the attic," who is the Baron's younger brother. Heloise is a Klopstock, and like Lister's attraction to his aunt Eleanor and the ambiguous sexuality of Passerat's friends, this increases the sense of inescapable entanglement and interchangeability of roles. Thus Eleanor and Lister "could be anybody, and more conceivably could be the master and mistress of the house just returned." Victor Passerat's name suggests change and unpredictability; that he is the guest "is not relevant. . . . It might be anybody," and his two friends "are killed instantly without pain" by lightning while they wait in the storm. In short, no human being is ever totally in absolute control, and the unexpected is all that one can really expect.

Indiscriminate sexuality, perhaps the most visible feature of contemporary life and a frequent interest in Spark's novels, is combined here with the idea that "sex" is "the forbidden word," "not to be mentioned." Lister says, "To do so would be to belittle their activities. On their [the Klopstocks] sphere sex is nothing but an overdose of life. They will die of it, or rather to all intents and purposes have died." In *Not to Disturb*, narrow self-interest directed to immediate satisfaction is the typical reason for behavior. The drawing room of the Klopstocks, notable for its many objects (including the family portraits) that "are on a miniature scale," reflects the quality of their owners' narrowly restricted and acquisitive lives. Although there are still possible alternatives to the kind of life the Klopstocks live, these seem few, a paucity that is appropriate to the dark world of these novels.

Since almost anyone could be the father of Heloise's child, she does not appear a discriminating individual, but her pregnancy gives her an extra resource of intuition that elicits from Lister a grudging respect. And just outside the center of action, there are others whose lives are less exploitative. The porter Theo and his wife Clara—whom the Baroness would dismiss—live apart from the manor and do not fully enter into its life. Clara "looks as if she were steady of mind but she says, 'I think I am going mad.' " Terrible dreams disturb her, she lacks facile sexual responses, she is frightened by a scandal, and she is distressed when Lister is "no different from usual." Clara's concern about Lister's callousness is aberrant behavior at the Klopstock Chateau, where the domestic staff complacently dine and prepare their stories for the press while murders are committed. "By noon they will be covered in the profound sleep of those who have kept faithful vigil all night, while outside the house the sunlight is laughing on the walls."

The future Klopstocks, promiscuous Heloise and mad sex-crazed "him in the attic," provide a grotesque commentary. At the wedding, the bridegroom rips the zip-fastener from his jump suit, dances free, and lustily falls upon his pregnant wife, as sound and film-track record the event. And, it is observed, "He was only doing his thing." This cliché is used early in the novel when Lister asks about those who are locked in the library:

"What were they doing anyway, amongst us, on the crust of this tender earth?" he says. "What were they doing here?"

The other servants fall silent. "What are they doing here, anyway, in this world?"

Heloise, pink and white of skin, fresh from her little sleep, says, "Doing their own thing."

Such exclusive concern with self-indulgence shows an extreme poverty of humanity and perhaps explains both the relentless exploitations of mass media and sexuality. When sensationalism is the all of existence, it appears purposeless. The vision of Barbara Vaughan, who recognized that "With God everything is possible," is far beyond people like Eleanor, who notes, "When you say a thing is not impossible, that isn't quite as if to say it's possible. . . . Only technically is the not impossible, possible," or Lister and Pablo who speak of facts accomplished. The widespread occurrence of feelings of futility reflects a waning of belief and the corollary of desperate attempts at control. But a faithless reality leads to extraordinary role-playing in a world where terror pervades and man is seen in terms of miniatures. Murder is merely a fact, a curiosity, to be turned to profit by the skilled opportunist. Since the victims are self-chosen, charitable concern is not required.

Muriel Spark used many of her favorite materials—suspense, the grotesque, meticulous details, poetic elegance, a single event to serve as catalyst for reevaluation—but here, as in the previous two novels, she shaped them somewhat differently. Her attack is upon a broad spectrum of inhumanity rather than individual aberrancy. God is not recognized in this world of sham and self-delusion, a world that is so unmistakeably that in which we live. The earlier heroines, who necessarily lack complete understanding and yet recognize something beyond the immediate reality, are certainly more agreeable and reassuring. Spark's harsh starkness in these three novels is fearsome and reflects the prevailing tone, which can be modified only by a conversion to something beyond worldly interests. The darkening vision was not encouraging. In these books, Spark's sensitive response to an increasingly crass and indifferent world was to delineate it so sharply that the reader is denied an easy response. Spark achieved "the *desegregation* of art—the liberation of our minds from the comfortable cells of lofty sentiment."[8] Having managed this, she returned in the next novels to a somewhat less severe mode.

9

Purgatorial Uneasiness

The Hothouse by the East River

Living in an apartment building near the United
Nations, Muriel Spark was at work as early as 1965 on
a novel about New York; in an interview she gave its
working title as "Hothouse East River."[1] The genesis of
the ideas for *The Hothouse by the East River* was thus
closer to that of *The Mandelbaum Gate* than to the
preceding three novels. Both, for example, involved
British intelligence and spies. Other similarities were a
longer period of composition and a marked change in
style.

The novel's experimental quality is reflected in the
opening line, "If only it were true that all's well that
ends well, if only it were true." The use of the conditional sets a mood that is speculative and tentative.
Questions are raised without being answered, and
reversals occur frequently. Nevertheless, the novel is
splendidly precise in its evocation of time and space.
The present tense is used throughout, so that all of the
action is immediately before one's eyes.

The immediate setting is Manhattan in the 1970s.
Paul and Elsa Hazlett, upper-middle class, wealthy,
and sophisticated expatriots, move through "New
York, home of the vivisectors of the mind, and of the
mentally vivisected still to be reassembled, of those

who live intact, habitually wondering about their states of sanity and home of those whose minds have been dead, bearing the scars of resurrection. . . ."

Elsa's analyst, Garven Bey, is temporarily serving as her butler to document her history and prevent her return to a clinic. His analyst, Annie Armitage, shadows Elsa to know details of the case. They all meet like civilized people; the two analysts become lovers and professional partners to advance their cases. "It's the secondary associative process of the oblique approach" is Spark at her satiric best.

Indeed, the New York material is often devastating and hilarious. Psychologist Annie Armitage lists "serious problems" that include everything. She is interrupted finally when Elsa observes through her window facing the United Nations, a demonstration of nude policemen, identifiable only by their caps, who are seeking, according to the placards they carry, "JUSTICE FOR US COPS." The list of patients' disorders includes "schizophrenia of the pancreas," "libidinal spleen," and "a manic-depressive kidney." The Hazletts' son Pierre stages a geriatric production of *Peter Pan* in Greenwich Village. This is enthusiastically received with a comment that epitomizes the United States in the 1970s: "Sick is interesting. Sick is real." Pierre's philosophical summation states the problem explicitly: "There's only one area of conflict left and that's between absurdity and intelligence."[2] The mind, then, is Spark's center in *The Hothouse by the East River*.

The narrative plot in New York is sparse and simple. The Hazletts, an older couple, meet a few people—their analysts, Bey and Armitage; their children, Pierre and Katerina; an old friend from their life in wartime Britain, Princess Poppy Xavier; and Helmet Kiel, a German they knew in 1944 and now a shoe salesman, with whom Elsa makes a trip to Zurich. Paul and Elsa compare their present in a hot apartment in one of "those high steel structures" with the time when they were twenty-eight and twenty-three and working in "the green depths of England." The early years of the Hazletts' lives are central to a secondary plot, which receives less space but is no less important to the novel.

In the early spring of 1944, during the Second World War, Elsa and Paul work outside London for a branch of British Intelligence. They are part of the Compound where, with German prisoners of war who have agreed to collaborate, they engage in "black propaganda and psychological warfare. This is the propagation of the Allied point of view under the guise of the German point of view; it involves a tangled mixture of damaging lies, flattering and plausible truths." Such creation of fiction is, of course, acceptable because it is part of a larger truth, the defense against the patent evils of the Axis powers. Indeed, a major point of difference between the world of the 1970s and wartime Britain is the clear sense of purpose. Whatever the dangers and horrors of World War II, there was no ambiguity about the rightness of the cause, "when people were normal and there was a world war on . . . life was more vivid. . . . Everything was more distinct. . . . One lived excitedly and dangerously."

During the war, Paul contrasts the "appalling" nature of "burrowing like a mole with secret work" to the "rattle and bash" of being "in an armoured car in a convoy," a part of the visible army. He remains uneasy, a normal condition for an intelligence person. The Hazletts are Spark's addition to the familiar figures of the spy thriller, the twentieth century's distinctive fictional form, notable for exploring existential themes.[3] Agents characteristically put their fantasies into action by creating new identities, playing a variety of roles, and inevitably being suspicious and uncertain. Thus Paul thinks that Elsa is sleeping with prisoner Helmet Kiel, the SS officer he accuses of being a double agent and who is shot while trying to escape. This is a world in which absurdity and intelligence are often indistinguishable, a world of shadows.

The shadow is a fundamental metaphor in *Hothouse.* The first hint about the real subject of the novel comes after three pages, when Paul looks at his wife's shadow and sees it, as he has "many times before, cast once more unnaturally," so that there is darkness where light should be. Discerned even in photographs, Elsa's shadow is noted more than twenty times. The shadow is an important sign, as any reader of Dante's *The Divine Comedy* knows. When that poet visited Purgatorio, only he cast a shadow among the shades, who were perturbed by this indication that he was of a different order. Elsa is similarly identified as a being set apart, one "who gets light or something from elsewhere." In contrast to Paul, she seems in a state of expectancy. Her looking out across the East River at something that is visible to no one else, is an anticipation of "the Nothing beyond the window." In Christian iconography a church must be situated so that the altar faces the rising sun, a looking to the East for resurrection.

Spark's novel has many allusions that suggest an allegory of souls in Purgatory. Imagery of the grave and physical corruption appear throughout *The Hothouse by the East River.* Paul is constantly adding ice to his drink: this is a response to the "hot" house, but is also a sign of his frozen quality and a way of recalling that Satan in Dante's *Inferno* is in ice. Early in the novel, Paul's thumping heart is described as "battering the sides of the coffin," and at the end "His heart knocks on the sides of the coffin." He charges Elsa to "go back to the grave from where I called you." Elsa refers to "this deadly body of mine" as "in full health, dusting the dust away," and says it "can dance, too." Most startlingly, Princess Poppy Xavier has the habit of keeping the eggs of her silkworms warm by placing them in the folds of her breasts. In the heat the eggs hatch into worms that wriggle upon her breast. This vivid image is like a medieval *memento mori*. Modern psychologist Garven screams when he beholds it and repeats "Don't panic" to those who are in fact not disturbed.

Several passages state that what appears is not necessarily reality: there is a questioning of facts, a recognition of illusion, an argument that what is believed in becomes reality, that what is being said does not really matter, and that the characters themselves are not real but rather a development of Paul's idea of them. Only at the end of the novel are we told explicitly that the events in New York—having a job at Columbia and living in the apartment of Paul's friend Molly—are what might have happened, had the principals lived. Actually Elsa and Paul, along with Poppy Xavier, Colonel Tylden, and Miles Bunting, were in the back section of a train that was completely demolished by a direct hit of a V-2 rocket bomb in the late spring of 1944.

Knowing this, we understand Spark's intention in *The Hothouse by the East River* more clearly. A crosscutting of action from 1944 Britain to 1970s New York shows the limitations of immersion in material time. In a larger scheme (the view beyond the East River), either period is trivial. The "vivisection of the mind" that takes place in New York is far more than Spark's witty surgical exploration of society; it is an imaginative exploration of the passing from this life to afterlife.

The novel is filled with bizarre and grotesque characters and situations, but typically there is a serious point. To describe Paul and Elsa's final evening in New York, for example, Spark uses both playful extravaganza and a metaphor of pilgrimage. They move from place to place, beginning appropriately with a nightspot called the Personality Cult and proceeding to a golden wedding anniversary party, to dinner with friends, to discotheques called The Sensual Experience and Roloff's. At the last spot Elsa and Paul create a sensation dancing under psychedelic lights because of Elsa's shadow. Everyone believes that there is a trick, and the proprietor wants to sign them up for a nightly floor show. This is at once hilarious and terrifying—aging wouldbe swingers and a literal Dance of Death. Or more simply, it is an observation of how little is understood when again absurdity and intelligence are the only choices.

In an early scene Elsa upsets her therapist by quoting Saint Augustine: "I came to Carthage . . . where there bubbled around me in my ears a cauldron of unhappy loves."[4] In Spark's anagogic view, blending theology and metaphor, the "hot house" of the title is both the Hazletts' apartment and the city in which they live and also, as the shadow image indicates, Purgatory. Literally, the apartment is hot, in a July summer or in the winter when the central heating cannot be adjusted. There is also lust, Paul's sexual jealousy and Elsa's infidelity. Lust appears also in the sterility of their children's sexuality, for Pierre is a homosexual and Katerina a prostitute. However, just as Augustine did not remain forever abandoned to a life of pleasure, so the Hazletts pass through Purgatory.

As presented by Muriel Spark, Purgatory is remarkably like life on this earth, a depressing continuation, which is comparable to Jean Paul Sartre's Hell in *No Exit*. Paul is as anxious as he was in London, seeking to create and control, and thus perpetuating his own uncertainty and unhappiness. In short, he is another of Spark's disturbing willful characters who cannot accept life for what it is but must write it their own way. Tired of being patient and sweet, Elsa wants to move on; she insists with increasing intensity that Paul recognize they died in the 1944 bombing. This is a first stage of a freeing from attachment to the world.

The difficulty of her task is underscored by Paul's insistence that she is mad, has departed from reason. Annie Armitage observes curtly, "The hell with her shadow." Paul supports the analyst to confirm his own judgment. The labeling of Elsa's malady as schizophrenia reflects the recent psychological theory that to be mad in the eyes of the world, to withdraw from it, is the only sanity in an absurd present world. Paul recognizes painfully that he is on a different plane from Elsa; he is "only a little figure far below her and her thoughts."

The Hothouse by the East River chronicles the existence of those who are dead but still seeking answers to questions. The opening conditional statement, "If only it were true that all's well that ends well," is restated toward the conclusion by a declaration that "One should live first, then die, not die then live, everything in its own time." This is a wish not to be in the purgatory stage but rather to have understood while alive, to have grown up properly, not to be a Peter Pan.

Paul is, of course, similar to Peter Pan, the boy who stays in Never-Never Land, where there is also difficulty about a shadow. But Elsa is not willing to play Wendy. While all others applaud Pierre's geriatric production at the Very Much Club, Elsa waits for the traditional scene of the Island of Lost Boys. Then she throws soft tomatoes at the actors, especially Peter. This is both comic absurdity and literary criticism, but is is also a theological rejection: Peter Pan's refusal to grow old is a rejection of the essential human condition. He refuses to leave the known limits to gain the limitless possibilities; theologically this is analogous to grasping only the temporal, never growing beyond its limitations to the eternal God. Pierre's over-sixty cast grotesquely shows the ridiculousness of protracted youth, another salient quality of American culture that Spark is satirizing.

The contrast of Old and New World, familiar theme of Henry James, is also parodied by Spark. To "Green England" is attributed the innocence that James gave to the United States; the Europeans, dead and suspended in New York, are indistinguishable from the natives, though Elsa claims to have been "far out" for longer. Spark's shifts of meaning, her inversions of traditional expectations, make *The Hothouse by the East River* a delight for those who like to play games of literary identification.

The micro effect of inverted ages in *Peter Pan* prepares us for the macro reversal of the form with which Spark is here experimenting, the anti-novel. Her declared admiration for contemporary French authors like Robbe-Grillet is here expressed through her use of some of the techniques of the anti-novel—narrative through the present tense and through an external view, dialogue that shows the sickness within. The intention of the anti-novelist is to present life as absurd. Spark, however, is concerned with the crucial choice between absurdity and intelligence, and she chooses the latter.

Intelligence, moreover, is defined in an unexpected way. The last line of the novel describes Paul's following Elsa, "watching as she moves how she trails her faithful and lithe cloud of unknowing across the pavement." This is the culmination of the shadow image. Earlier Elsa's shadow signaled that she was in a different state from everyone else. Not all of those killed in the train in 1944 are thus set apart. Spark's intention seems to have been far more than a suggestion of a soul in purgatory, a condition that the Hazletts share.

What distinguishes Elsa is her understanding, the

nature of which is made explicit by the phrase "trails her faithful and lithe cloud of unknowing." To Freddy Hamilton in *The Mandelbaum Gate* events came back "like a cloud of unknowing, heavy with the molecules of accumulated impressions." Though he finally discerns that he has behaved well, the transfiguration is "without any disastrous change in the appearance of things." In contrast, Elsa's "cloud of unknowing" is described as "faithful" and "lithe," and she "trails" it. This means a permanent assimilation that is graceful and supple, not a momentary perception. The precision of verbal nuance also reminds us that Spark is a poet-novelist.

The fourteenth-century mystical treatise *The Cloud of Unknowing* is a guide to contemplation. When Elsa sits quietly by the window, she is utterly detached from those around her; she is in contemplation. This is a time of awareness of God, a knowing and loving at the core of one's being that comes only with a basic sense of "otherness," to which the soul turns as its own. The "cloud of unknowing" is that darkness of intellectual ignorance that covers God, and which can be penetrated only through the constant pressure of love. The life of the contemplative is unknowing knowing, and Spark conveys this in Elsa.

Elsa's serenity and separateness disturb those around her, for she obviously knows what they do not perceive. She puts aside the human terms of her existence to see the No-thing and No-where that is God. Unlike Peter Pan's Never-Never Land or Paul's continuing preoccupation with the things of this world (like his wife's infidelity), Elsa's knowing and loving God is self-less. By remaining with Paul she has served as his spiritual mentor.

At the end of the novel, they are free from the "hothouse"; the upper stories of the apartment building have already been knocked out by the demolition crew, as Elsa and Paul turn in another direction. Elsa notes, "Now we can have some peace," and Paul admits that everyone's "been very patient, really." Solipsism has been replaced by a recognition of otherness, when Paul grows beyond petty self-interest. It is true that "all's well that ends well"; the fall of man is followed by Christ's Incarnation, and after the Crucifixion man is redeemed. However, it is also true that Purgatory is a stage on the pilgrim's way to God.

The Abbess of Crewe

When it was published in 1974, *The Abbess of Crewe* achieved more notoriety than most of Spark's preceding novels. It carried the subtitle "a modern morality tale," but this discreet pointing was unnecessary. Allegorical intention and satirical commentary about the Watergate Affair were obvious. For months the world press had reported details about the break-in at Democratic headquarters in Washington, D.C., and the subsequent cover-up that eventually led to the resignation of Richard M. Nixon as President of the United States on August 9, 1974. Spark got the idea for *The Abbess of Crewe* while reading a newspaper in Ceylon; in an interview, she noted her fascination with "how Watergate blew up from nothing."[4]

The Abbess of Crewe provokes wicked laughter; but since topicality quickly becomes less pertinent and amusing, it is fortunate that the novella is more than political satire. Presenting a Watergate type scandal inside a Catholic abbey in England was an effective way of investigating a small group of people who live in a confined world and have little touch with outside reality. Again Spark used a singular focus to explore favorite themes—power, deception, corruption, solipsism—and to comment pointedly about shifting modes of modern Christianity.

There is an expectant air at the Benedictine Abbey of Crewe, where a successor of the late Abbess Hildegarde is to be elected. The likely choice is Sister Alexandra, a tall, slender, beautiful, pale aristocrat whose passion is English poetry. Alexandra is determined to maintain both ancient Benedictine traditions and a complex electronic system. She is regal in manner, authoritative in command, utterly convinced of her own righteousness, and absolutely certain that it is her "destiny" to be the new Abbess.

However, there is a rival, Sister Felicity, who advocates a Franciscan way of "total dispossession and love" and for whom "the point of faith is visibly to benefit mankind." She wants to turn Crewe into a "love-Abbey"; her passion is a Jesuit seminarian. Felicity is very bourgeois; her "treasured toy" is a tidy sewing box, elegantly fitted and containing a false bottom for love letters.

The rivals are, of course, caricatures of extreme Catholic views held both before and after the Second Vatican Council. They are also both examples of the excessive romanticism that Spark presents as dangerously destructive.

Sister Alexandra's two close confederates are Sister Mildred, the Novice Mistress, and Sister Walburga, the Prioress. In addition, Sister Winifrede, "the absolute and benighted clot," mindlessly attends to her errands. Although there seems little doubt about Sister Alexandra's election, her two main supporters plot with two friendly Jesuits, Fathers Baudoin and Maximilian. The four plan to discredit Felicity by stealing the Jesuit's love letters and making them public.

Alexandra is, of course, discreetly absent while the conspiracy is planned. She is a reader of Machiavelli, whose *Art of War* and *The Discourses* provide useful guidance for the securing and holding of power. She also seeks political advice from Sister Gertrude, a

missionary for the abbey who hurtles about the Third
World but keeps in close touch via "the green line."

Direct communication is very simple, for the green
line is only part of an elaborate electronic system at the
Abbey. Justified as a means for instructing the novices
to meet the challenges of the modern world, its
primary function seems to be to serve Alexandra. The
system provides complete surveillance; even the
avenue of poplars is bugged. The main transmitter is
concealed in the statue of the Infant of Prague, which
is kept in the Abbess's parlor. This electronic equipment keeps Alexandra well informed of Felicity's trysts
with her lover, of her advocacy in the Abbey of the
joys of love and freedom, and of her increasing elec-
toral support.

Scheming becomes reality when two Jesuit
seminarians break in and, as proof of their skill, take
the thimble from Felicity's sewing box. During a
second breakin to secure the letters an alerted Felicity
catches them and calls the police. Scandal is avoided
through Alexandra's cool management and the incident is noted only in a small newspaper item.
Responding to Prioress Walburga's request that she
comment on the disturbances to the assembled nuns in
chapter hall, Alexandra speaks not of "sanctity and
holiness" but of decorum. The candidate chooses exactly "the right note" by appealing to their snobbery.
Alexandra contrasts how a lady—clearly herself, the
traditional figure in the Benedictine Abbey of
Crewe—and a bourgeois—obviously Sister
Felicity—behave. Alexandra is easily elected, for
"Novices and nuns alike, they're snobs to the core."

With Alexandra's "landslide victory" there is little
chance for Felicity's style of "freedom." She joins her
lover in London and makes "extraordinary
disclosures" that bring press and television to the Abbey. A coverup is urgently needed, and the ruling
group devise various "scenarios." Those caught in the

break-in require money: a jewel from the Infant of
Prague is sold, and Sister Winifrede arranges a
meeting for the payoff. Winifrede chooses the ladies'
room at Selfridge's, a large London department store,
where in mufti she meets the ex-seminarian, who
comes dressed as a woman. This absurdity is un-
detected. Alexandra protests such risk-taking, but the
faithful and stupid follower arranges the second
meeting in the gentlemen's lavatory at the British
Museum. She is arrested as a transvestite. The expected scapegoat has already signed a "confession of
her sins" for Alexandra, who anticipated disclosure.

Alexandra appears on television, dazzling the press
with a wonderful performance and no clear answers.
She simply indicates that all is an ecclesiastical matter.
However, as the novella ends, the Abbess of Crewe
must still answer to Rome. Confident that, with her
edited tapes, she will convince the authorities of her
righteous action, Alexandra sets out on a fine day. She
travels, of course, by surface; but she stands on the upper deck, a still figure in white who marvels at the
changing surface of sea billows.

The novella is a stream of outlandish episodes
recounted in a spirited, witty, and startling language
that heightens the mad proceedings. The text is replete
with images like "this corridor of meditation by the
secret police of poplars." Cool and elegant Alexandra
shifts from reciting eloquent English poetry to crisp
comments about Felicity's sexual habits or "To hell
with St. Francis." Sister Gertrude is Alexandra's "excellent nun, learned Hun," and represents Henry
Kissinger, Nixon's Secretary of State. In this most obvious parallel, Spark has Gertrude constantly giving
pithy advice amidst bustling about and negotiating.
Gertrude tells Alexandra, "A problem you solve . . . a
paradox you live with."

The Abbess of Crewe is built upon many paradoxes.
Alexandra insists that the nuns follow the complete,

the oldest Benedictine regimen of prayer—all the
Hours of the Divine Office, including those in the middle of the night. She also insists upon the most
sophisticated electronic equipment. She preaches
dedication, but she is simply self-serving, adjusting
tapes and exploiting others for her own gains. The Abbess and her friends privately enjoy paté and fine
chilled wine, and the robe of the Infant of Prague is
embellished with jewels from the nuns' dowries, but
meals in the refectory are made from cat and dog food.
All "live with paradoxes." Indeed, the monastic injunction "watch and pray" is itself paradoxical, as is
the Catholic novelist's capacity to remain faithful in
the midst of showing the Church's folly and to see her
fiction as a game, part of God's cosmic play.

The reiterated motto "be vigilant, be sober" serves
for the Abbey but also for the reader, whom Spark is
deliberately teasing. Artifice like Alexandra's may
mislead. In the Abbey there is so much foolishness and
frailty that Alexandra may, like Jean Brodie, appear a
charismatic leader to follow. The two are alike in their
wish to control the destinies of others, in their snobbery, and in their lack of perspective. But Alexandra's
role-playing is more advanced; she manipulates
deliberately.

Theatrical imagery pervades *The Abbess of Crewe*.
Waiting in the chapter hall to hear Alexandra, the
nuns look about "as if they were at the theatre waiting
for the curtain to go up," and she performs brilliantly.
The Abbess makes a very successful television broadcast; she calls for scenarios; her keeping and editing
the tape recordings is an "orchestration."

In an early speech Alexandra explains, "Here, in the
Abbey of Crewe, we have discarded history. We have
entered the sphere, dear Sisters, of mythology." After
the scandal has broken, she notes, "We are truly
moving in a mythological context. We are the actors;
the press and the public are the chorus." Again there is
a paradox: "Mythology is nothing more than history

garbled." A good scenario is a "garbled" one and "needs not be plausible, only hypnotic, like all good art." Nevertheless, the realm of mythology has limits; Gertrude warns, "you won't get the mythological approach from Rome. In Rome, they deal with realities." There is, then, a reality beyond the history and mythology of the world, and Alexandra ignores this.

Before setting out for Rome Alexandra deletes from the tapes her recitations of English poetry, mostly written in the language of the Reformation, for as Gertrude warns, "Rome will take anything, but English poetry, no." All "trivial, fond records" are thus "sedulously expurgated" from the final compilation that is entitled *The Abbess of Crewe*. Making deletions and answering to Rome are a mode of accommodation, but the evidence of Spark's work suggests that Alexandra's chameleonlike shifting will at last be stopped. In an early conversation with Gertrude, Alexandra asserts "the Abbess of Crewe continues to perform her part in the drama of *The Abbess of Crewe*. The world is having fun and waiting for the catharsis. Is this my destiny?" History and mythology become indistinguishable. In their last conversation, Alexandra declares, "I have become an object of art, the end of which is to give pleasure." This is Spark's artistic credo, but unlike Alexandra she recognizes that art is deception ("fiction is all lies") and thus ultimately to be renounced.

The last paragraph begins with a line from Shakespeare, Prospero's conclusion of the masque in *The Tempest*, "Our revels now are ended." After the dramatic performance, it is necessary to attend to the realities of the world. Manipulations at Crewe are a debased analogue of the magic practiced on Prospero's island. Shakespeare's hero uses the time of isolation penitentially, to improve himself so that he can become an effective leader to serve his people whom he had neglected in his selfishness. Alexandra's time at the Abbey, also an island from the rest of the world, only furthers her pride. There is no awareness of failure, let alone repentance. Alexandra's power is used not for truth but for deception; she utterly betrays the Benedictine ideal of the Abbot who shows his authority through service.

An alternative to the enclosed religious life is Gertrude's way, going out as a missionary and saving souls through conversion. But Gertrude's needed strength is denied her community; advice over the green line is no corrective to Alexandra's ego and dominance of the Abbey. Gertrude points out that the would-be-Abbess Alexandra should have helped her sister Felicity by destroying the love letters, not by trying to exploit them. Similarly, she has advice about how the Pope should heed the Second Vatican Council. Pronouncements are easier than implementations. As a lone worker, Gertrude escapes the realities of community life. Felicity's cozy view of all-loving-together is similarly evasive, for it is mere pleasure-seeking.

In short, the religious directions followed in the novella are all man-centered, not God-directed. There is, then, a special poignancy in the injunction "Be still, be watchful." In this modern morality tale, there has been little evidence of receptivity to God's Grace, which is a gift, not something achieved through man's efforts. The final image of *The Abbess of Crewe* compares the smooth billowing sea waves of Alexandra's Channel crossing to "that cornfield of sublimity which never should be reaped nor was ever sown, orient and immortal wheat." Seeing a connection between this world and God's grandeur is "marvelous," but, when compared with limitless eternity, even expansive beauty is diminished. There are absurdities at Crewe, but also a more cheerful sense of possibility that is conveyed through the author's high spirits. Muriel Spark has moved beyond the severity, murders, and destruction of her darkening vision. The hilarity has verged upon the hysterical, but from purgatory it is possible to ascend.

10

Rights and Wrongs

The Takeover

In *The Abbess of Crewe*, Muriel Spark explored the difficulty of distinguishing mythology and history, particularly in their making. This philosophical and moral problem in many ways dominated the 1970s, a period of uncertainty and sweeping change. *The Takeover* is a tale of these times. The issues are serious ones, but the novel is a very funny book, surpassing the playfulness of *The Abbess* with a form that is essentially comedy of manners and written in a style that permits authorial commentary as well as flawless dialogue.

Longer than her two most recent novels, *The Takeover* rivaled *The Mandelbaum Gate* in its use of specific contemporary history and most fully reflected Spark's knowledge and experience of living in Rome. However, *The Takeover* expanded beyond this specificity into direct exploration of the nature of mythology, because Spark centered her tale at Nemi.[1] Located in the Alban Hills southeast of Rome, there is a picturesque crater lake and a sacred wood, site of a temple of Diana. Sir James Frazer, Scottish classicist and anthropologist, whose masterpiece *The Golden Bough* (1890) has greatly influenced twentieth-century literature and psychology, centered his comparative study of religion upon the high priest who attended at Nemi. Frazer showed parallels between early beliefs and rites and Christianity, and Spark continued her countryman's exploration of similarities by describing modern cults and the decline of Catholicism.

The period covered in *The Takeover* is 1973–1975; the plot, as is characteristic in a comedy of manners, is less important than the world evoked. The action centers upon a small group of extraordinarily rich people and their immediate circle. A middle-aged American woman, whose ownership of houses at Nemi makes her the center of a group, has recently married an Italian aristocrat. Their lives of easeful elegance are threatened by world economic developments and by social unrest and crime in Italy. However, they continue to enjoy luxurious homes, art, and old friends who value soothing, romantic conversation and indulge a variety of sexual liaisons and more temperate appetites for food. They try to protect themselves against burglaries and exploitative acquaintances, are anxious and regretful, but dynamically stirred only by utmost extremity. The subplot presents a charismatic leader who, convinced of his divine origins in pagan myth, discreetly exploits others, quickly recruits a following, and creates a ritualistic cult. But the ex-patriot Englishman's "truth" is short-lived. At the climactic gathering of his elect followers, the self-anointed priest is challenged by the Christian Word, and in the resulting confusion his religious trappings are dismantled.

Spark's comedy of manners is of the stricter sort, a reflection on the fashions, manners, and outlooks of a sophisticated, rather artificial society. Her characteristic satiric manner is replaced by an almost gossipy style, and there is more humor than wit. A pervasive Mediterranean laziness almost obscures the hard truth that is the core of Spark's work. Things—art, houses, jewelry, money—all these earthly things pass away.

Modern man does not believe in God; nevertheless, he
is willing to believe not in nothing but in anything,
and thus cults are formed. However, just as
Christianity took over from pagan myths, so can the
New Testament triumph today.

The central character in *The Takeover* is Maggie, a
wealthy American in her late forties, whose effect is
"absolutely imperious in its demand for attention."
Always tasteful and moving easily, she has recently
married Berto di Tullio-Friole, an Italian Marchesse,
after divorcing her second husband, Ralph Radcliffe,
who had money but thought of nothing else. Maggie's
fortune is enormous: "Mysterious and intangible,
money of Maggie's sort was able to take lightning trips
round the world without ever packing its bags or
booking its seat on a plane." Her administrative
headquarters occupy "an entire floor of offices in a
New York block." Berto's assets are so extensive that he
never thinks of money, but rather of tradition,
beautiful art, and courteous living.

Wealth is a major theme in the novel, the title of
which most explicitly refers to altering global
economic circumstances. A time of inflation, soaring
oil prices, assets that could not be protected, "this last
quarter of the year they had entered, that of 1973, was
in fact the beginning of something new in their world;
a change in the meaning of property and money." Berto's observation that things will never be the same
reflects the conservative's alarm about the rash of
burglaries and kidnappings that occur daily in Italy
and an even greater anxiety about the election of the
Communists. The constant threat and reality of loss
are an unavoidable part of the wealthy Italian scene;
burglaries and kidnapping, as Spark described them,
are the material of current journalistic accounts.
Maggie responds hysterically to the theft of her jewelry
from a villa at Ischia, but she is more continuously involved in attempts to protect her property from those

she knows than from unknown intruders. Losing material objects seems less onerous than being taken advantage of.

Hubert Mallindaine, who for a time "took over" Maggie's life, continues to live in the new villa she built at Nemi, another form of takeover. It is one of three important houses and commands the finest view of the lake. The site is crucial to Hubert, who convinced Maggie to buy and supervised the improvements. Hubert believes and proclaims himself a descendant of Diana and the Roman Emperor Caligula, who took the goddess on his pleasure ship on the lake, through their child, who became a woodland priest. Hubert's bizarre, elaborate myth began with "a little story fostered by a couple of dotty aunts," who were enamored of Frazer's work and consulted a quack Victorian genealogist. Intelligent and charming, Hubert is penniless so that he exploits Maggie's wealth and careless generosity not only by living in her house but also by selling her antiques and a Gauguin painting, after substituting excellent fakes. He begins living in Nemi with four "secretaries," attractive young men, but gradually shifts his interest and energy to forming the Friends of Diana and Apollo. The cult of the Brothers and Sisters of Nature attracts many followers, including two American Jesuits, Fathers Gerald Harvey and Cuthbert Plaice. The latter has a special interest in ecology, and Spark's choice of names alerts us that there is something "fishy" about him.

This return to the worship of a pagan goddess amuses Hubert and provides a sense of power. He clothes himself as a priest, creates a ritual, and addresses the crowds charismatically. Indeed, his fanciful, emotional services are compared by Spark to the Charismatic Christians who gather at St. Peter's in Rome. The climax of the novel comes at Nemi when certain elect Friends are gathered to hear of "the old religion that goes back beyond the dawn of history, into the far and timeless regions of mythology where centuries and eons do not count." Hubert's carefully orchestrated sermon is interrupted by a cry of "I'm going to testify" from his secretary, Pauline Thin. A Catholic who had earlier warned Hubert not to insult her religion, she, like Saint Paul, introduces the New Testament to the assembled crowd. In this takeover she is supported by another Englishwoman, Nancy Cowan, tutor to the Bernardinis, who live in Maggie's largest house. Diana of Nemi is identified with Diana of Ephesus, the many-breasted pagan goddess against whom Saint Paul spoke. Hubert, with cadenced responses, tries to turn the charges to his advantage in a wildly parodic scene where Hubert's Italian lawyer, Massimo, provides antiphonal translations. The rally of the faithful turns into a rout.

Hubert's cult, "his hopes," are all over. Nevertheless, he has put aside money from the sale of Maggie's goods, and Pauline explains that Father Cuthbert wants him to take over the Charismatic Movement in the Church and run the prayer meetings. This would not be a conflict with Diana, the Lady of Wildlife—an outrageous Sparkian pun—so that Hubert "hasn't done so badly." Final removal from Nemi comes, however, not from the fiasco of the last gathering but through the Byzantine intricacies of the Italian legal system. One of Hubert's "secretaries" in his first year at Nemi was Lauro, a slim handsome youth who left Hubert to work for Maggie's son Michael and his wife Mary. Lauro is ambitious and adaptable. He satisfies the sexual interests not only of Maggie and Mary but also of Berto and Michael, Maggie's husband and son. The maid Agota is pregnant with his child, but he marries his fiancée, a sturdy middle-class girl named Elisabetta, after learning that the land at Nemi—ten acres on the plateau—actually belongs to her. Lauro is delighted that he can take over from his employers. Maggie was duped with false title deeds, and thus all the buildings were illegally constructed. In Italian law, Maggie's three houses are *abusiro*; they do not exist.

Substantial wealth, then, may instantly become insubstantial. Maggie's global fortune also disappears; she entrusts its management to Coco de Renault, an Argentinian financier who happened to visit at Berto's Palladian villa. Busy with her social life and getting Hubert out of her house, Maggie does not notice how Coco is taking over. But when she realizes that her funds are stopped and her office disbanded, she hunts for Coco through Switzerland. Maggie, who is very pragmatic, views her fortune according to present circumstances in Italy. She enlists Lauro's aid and arranges to have Coco kidnapped, so that she can demand a huge ransom: "Why shouldn't I be a criminal? Everyone else is!" In fact, she will recover her fortune—less thirty percent, the kidnappers' share.

Maggie rather enjoys the exercise of being driven about Switzerland attending to criminal arrangements. She stops at a flea market to buy strange clothes and "dresses up as a pauper because she wants everyone to know that she is ruined." Nevertheless, Maggie remains "still handsome and gleaming through it all." Thus she appears to Berto at the villa, and to Hubert, whom she meets again at Nemi, where the kidnapped Coco is being held in a cave until the ransom is paid. The status quo will be preserved, and Coco will not dare to indict Maggie because, "He's too indictable himself."

The rich and the crooks are very similar in the ways of *The Takeover*; both are part of a zany round that seems always turning. The original myth of the priesthood of Diana involved a takeover. The priest was always a murderer, one who gained his position by slaying the previous priest. In a milder form of ritual at Nemi only a runaway slave who had broken off a branch of a certain tree, the Golden Bough, was entitled to the single combat to become the new priest. This custom was preserved into imperial times. Spark's Lauro, whose name is unusual for a Christian, perhaps is the modern descendant of the priest, since the golden bough may be a laurel. Lauro achieves the takeover at Nemi when he acquires the area through marriage. He is not a slave, but he begins as a servant. Lauro, whose name suggests *loro* (them), resents this role, the modern equivalent for slave; he protests with an expectation of something better awaiting him. The other three "secretaries," encouraged by Maggie, threaten to kill Hubert, although this is never seriously intended. In the modern materialistic world, the real loss is property, not life.

The absence of murder or death is an important feature in *The Takeover*, for it is very much a novel about survival. The stress is upon coping in the contemporary world. The capacity to survive is seen most clearly in Maggie and Hubert, but the two are very different.

Maggie's extraordinary wealth makes her a special person. However, as Berto observes, she is "A wonderful woman, a wonderful woman. She doesn't need money to make a her a wonderful woman. It's only that she's used to it." Indeed, though Maggie has the careless indifference to money that only the rich can afford, she is also aware of moral dimensions. She rents the largest of her villas at Nemi to Emilio Bernardini "in an access of financial morality" because this regularizes her investment at Nemi. She wants to be rid of Hubert, yet she anonymously sends him a valuable coin collection, thus providing financial means but not a continued formal tie. She accepts Coco de Renault as a financier with the trusting indifference of the Italian aristocracy; but, when her suspicions of his duplicity are confirmed, she fiercely takes action to recover her fortunes. Hubert deplores her "lack of chivalry" in not making him a settlement, but Maggie's resistance to exploitation is precisely what makes her attractive. Thus the leftist lawyer Massimo "loathed what he conceived Maggie to stand for at the same time as he was put into an ambivalent state of excitement by her glowing and wealthy presence." This is a characteristic positive response to Maggie, though she is once literally "burned" by some of Hubert's homosexual friends at a Bohemian party.

Maggie is not a philanthropist; however, she never controls other people, and she is utterly without pretension. She survives through a basic toughness, acknowledging her own failures and those of others. Occasionally impatient and angry, she usually remains detached. The final scene at Nemi epitomizes her resilience. She laughs at her crone-like appearance, recognizing its advantages in evading the notice of kidnappers who prey upon the rich. Maggie moves along the leafy path with only the light of a flashlight and the moon. The illumination is not dazzling, but adequate for Maggie to make her way to "the kindly fruits of the earth."

Hubert, in contrast, demands splendor. He exults in proclaiming himself divine. At Nemi he shouts, "It's mine! I am the King of Nemi! It is my divine right! I am Hubert Mallindaine the descendant of the Emperor of Rome and the Benevolent-Malign Diana of the Woods." The name Mallindaine is derived from the old french *malline* meaning "malign" and Diane with the "i" and "a" reversed to conceal the pagan origin of the name, so the family could avoid Church opposition. Maggie and Mary do not think Hubert evil, but "a bum." This view is modified for the reader when Hubert, having taken money to help Kurt, abandons this ex-"secretary," almost insensible with drugs, on the Spanish Steps in Rome. Further, Hubert preaches: "Truth is not literally true. The literal truth is a common little concept, born of the materialistic mind." This is reminiscent of Jean Brodie's elitism, though she was never greedy for money. Hubert's brilliant assumed sacerdotal robes contrast with Maggie's drab pauper's garb; both are outward signs of inner qualities.

In the words of Luke's Gospel (6:20), the first Beatitude of the Sermon on the Mount is: "Blessed are you poor, for yours is the kingdom of God." *The Takeover* is not about people who are poor in this world's goods. Alike in a basic greed, all of them secure material things, and there is no exception. This relentless exploitation is shown in the Jesuit priests, who constantly cadge a meal or invitation; in Lauro, who takes sex, gold, and land; in the scheming financier Coco, who steals Maggie's fortune; and in Hubert, who most values in life hope and drama—"all things being equal on the material side."

Spark's fiction creates the material reality of 1973–1975 in and about Rome, where history and mythology have blended for centuries. But all of this is really insubstantial: Hubert is right when he says that "literal truth is a common little concept, born of the materialistic mind," but his claim and his cult are what he decries.

The characters in the novel lack the perception that Spark gives the reader in a long authorial comment, of great poetic beauty, which introduces the idea of something beyond "the kindly fruits of the earth" so associated with Diana of Ephesus.[2] Two minor characters, Agata and her friend Clara, stand "in the sunny main street of Nemi," talking,

while life bustled by them . . . while the whole of eternal life carried on regardless, invincible and implacable . . . eternal life untraceable and persistent, that not even the excavators, long-dead, who had dug up the fields of Diana's sanctuary had found; they had taken away the statues and the effigies, . . . but eternal life had never been shipped off with the lost . . . that eternal life which remained, past all accounting.

With eternal life there is no takeover; the material that is measured by accounting, is transcended. Even Hubert admits that Maggie's style denotes a "need for stability and order" and her appearance achieves harmony; her "plans" denote a recognition of something future. Maggie's appearance as a pauper at Nemi is an image of apotheosis. What Hubert has done, she accepts, just as she earlier recognized "her impotence in territorial rights." Spark continued to ask what anyone can claim, and this is a major theme in the next novel, *Territorial Rights*.

Territorial Rights

Many stories in the Italian press during the 1970s dealt with the economy. In *The Takeover*, Muriel Spark explored the lives of the very rich, those who are constantly in danger of kidnapping and burglary and whose misadventures are the subject of popular journalism. *Territorial Rights* continued this investigation with a shift in location from Rome to Venice. There is a corollary of heightened materialist interest, for Venice's glory was created through commercial enterprise not always influenced by religious or moral concern. Mythology is not a deep root in Venice's tradition; instead, there is a romantic aura and golden light, captured in both mosaics and paintings, that can quickly darken. This is not a world for comedy of manners. Thus Spark returns to the techniques of the thriller, counterpointing a grizzly murder from the time of the Nazi occupation with present-day evil, and to the ingenious plotting of devious blackmail and theft.

The story begins thirty-five years before the main action of *Territorial Rights*. Victor Pancev, a minor official at the Bulgarian court, disappears on the funeral day of King Boris, amidst rumors that the occupying Germans instigated the poisoning of the king.

Pancev is seen in Venice, and a message is sent to his wife, but he never returns home. Pancev stays at the Villa Sofia with a Bulgarian count who dies a natural death, but the fugitive Victor is killed. Two servants, Katerina and Eufemia, report that Victor was found dead in the garden and his body "taken away." They inherit the villa, supposedly as the Count's illegitimate daughters. Victor has a daughter, Lina, born after he left Bulgaria.

Lina grows up under the Communists without an interest in her past, but she is fascinated by a visiting cousin's tale of life in decadent bourgeois London. A successful artist and teacher, Lina finally visits Paris and defects to the West. After some notoriety and a trip to London, Lina becomes just another displaced person, uncertain about ideology, penniless, without territoral rights. She decides to go to Venice to search for her dead father.

In Paris Lina meets a young Englishman, Robert Leaver, who is a student of art history. His father, Arnold, is headmaster of Ambrose College, and his mother, Anthea, is a disciplined woman who suffers her husband's infidelities, glosses over the idea of her son's homosexuality, and reads popular novels. Robert is the lover of Mark Curran, a sixty-two-year-old, extraordinarily rich, American art connoisseur and dealer, who provides Robert with security, rich presents, and elegant surroundings. Perhaps it is Lina's very shabbiness and uncertainty that attract Robert. He is fascinated by her life-style: her territorial rights are a jumble of rubbishy items and a cheap rented single room. Robert follows her to Venice, and his going brings others.

Mark Curran, who knows Venice well, wants a better parting than the "goodbye, goodbye, goodbye, good*bye*" he managed when the floundering Robert left him. Curran stays in the luxury Hotel Lord Byron, but Robert goes to the Pensione Sofia, a small

establishment run by Eufemia and Katerina and not
unknown to Curran. Also booked there are Robert's
father and Mary Tiller, an ex-cookery teacher from the
school, who is now his mistress. Last to arrive at the
Pensione Sofia is Grace Gregory, Arnold's former
mistress, a retired school matron. Distinguishing between "adultery" and "fornication," Grace wants to
assure that the wayward husband returns to her friend
Anthea. Leo, a former favorite student and now her
young protégé, accompanies Grace. He is of Italian
and Jewish heritage.

Beyond the confines of the Pensione Sofia and the
Hotel Lord Byron is the Ca' de Winter, decaying pal-
ace of Violet, an English expatriot. A friend of Curran
since the War days, Violet was, like Katerina and
Eufemia, Pancev's mistress. She now supplements her
income by working for GESS (Global-Equip Security
Services), an organization that investigates a variety of
cases. GESS ignores others' territorial rights; it covers,
"if the job's big enough, any territory in the world." In
a   cheaper   part   of   Venice   there   is   also   a
butcher's shop run by Giorgio, the assistant of the
"Butcher" who once rendered services at the Pensione
Sofia when Pancev died.

The plot, then, always comes back to the murdered
Bulgarian, whose grave Robert succeeds in finding.
Giorgio, "a talent spotter," recognizes the young
man's criminal potential and recruits him to blackmail
Curran by staging a false kidnapping and demanding
ransom. He knows what happened to Pancev as well as
the connections of Curran and Violet de Winter to the
Pensione Sofia.

Some of the details of the Pancev case are supplied
by Giorgio; others come from the imagination of
Robert, who writes them as the outline for a novel,
into which he also introduces fact and fiction about
the lives of Mary Tiller and Grace Gregory. To suppress the Pancev story, Curran, who is "rich

enough to take an objective point of view in a case where he's involved," pays Giorgio $100,000. This tidy sum is in addition to the half million dollars he pays to GESS. The GESS agent, Mr. B., learned of Curran's involvement with Robert through Anthea's attempt to find her missing son. Marital infidelity of a poor man is of no interest, but Violet is ordered by the Big Five at GESS to arrange an appropriate payoff from the wealthy Curran.

Improbable conjunctions of people and coincidences were not unusual for Spark, though the groups in other novels were less diverse. In the midst of the bizarre circumstances in Venice, Grace Gregory reports back to Anthea by telephoning England. In the abandoned wife's tidy and disciplined, albeit oppressive, world, "It all sounds very far-fetched." Grace's reply, "It may seem far-fetched to you . . . but here everything is stark realism. This is Italy," can stand as an apology for *Territorial Rights*.

As always, Spark's plotting is careful. The garden, for example, is constantly and menacingly present. Eufemia and Katerina are seen quarreling over where leaves fall in their clearly divided garden long before we learn how Victor Pancev's body was divided for burial there. Robert's hideous moment of evil triumph comes when he succeeds in having Lina, with whom he has not shared his knowledge, literally dance upon her father's grave. This is a fulfillment of an earlier conversation in which Lina had tried to soften Robert's feelings about his father's sexual misadventures. To her strong claim "your father is your flesh and your blood; if he was in his grave you would look for the grave like me," Robert says, "I would dance on it." Having discarded Lina for Anna, Giorgio's protégé, Robert gets his Bulgarian former mistress to the garden. From the canal, Anna's voice directs Lina to dance on the special rose beds which cover her father. The macabre situation is further enhanced for Robert because Lina is accompanied by his father, Arnold, who joins her in a delighted and somewhat drunken dance. Lina recognizes Robert's laugh and thinks that he is showing off for his new girlfriend. Not knowing that she is dancing on her father's grave, Lina believes she will humiliate Robert by dancing with his father.

Robert's evil is most carefully delineated in *Territorial Rights*. He is at the center not only because all the characters converge in Venice through knowing him, but also because the novel chronicles his development. As a boy at his father's school, Robert was a snoop; he was a whore in Paris before forming his allegiance with Curran, whom he abandons when Lina interests him. Everything leads to his being spotted by the deliberate criminals in Italy. He joins Giorgio and Anna with excitement, thinking, "I could be walking into a trap." But he proves "a marvel," one "born to the trade"; he knows "with a rush of pleasure: At last I'm home—I'm out of the trap." Preparing the blackmail material is "the most heavenly experience he had ever known," and this activity alternates with making love to Anna. During this time of bliss, Robert does not even distinguish the days.

From this "beginning of Robert's happy days, the fine fruition of his youth," there is no stopping. After Giorgio gets rid of them, Anna and Robert go to Verona and skillfully manage their first jewel robbery. Again "a talent spotter" makes contact, and their criminal career develops quickly. After a bank robbery, the newspaper carries the story of "I Bonnie e Clyde d'Italia." There is always another "talent spotter," and Spark explains in the concluding chapter that Anna and Robert go on the "to the Middle East to train in a terrorist camp."

Terrorists are the ultimate violators of territorial rights, for they destroy people and property indiscriminately. Robert is part of the student population that will "provoke a riot for a refused telephone call." Curran notes how deliberately Robert wants to make him feel "old and wicked," and the blackmail is a denial of his right to privacy or property. Yet Robert's behavior makes clear that he himself will not be interfered with; his mother is frightened to leave a telephone message for him, lest he think she is interfering. Similarly, Lina moves from place to place, never having a loyalty except to her own self-interest. She returns to Bulgaria with Serge, as a "first-rate example of a repentant dissident," and exploits her re-defection as selfishly as her time in the West. Care for others or belief in values is not evident.

The older generation have a different sense of territorial rights. While noting his own youth, Curran yet contrasts having "some sense of behaviour" and "feeling" with people like Robert and Lina, who "don't care what happens to their friends, they just fall into bed with someone else." Some residual sense of responsibility makes him follow Robert, arrange a job for Lina with Violet, pay blackmail. Arnold also looks for his son and "returns to his own territory." Anthea fells possessive about her husband and son and breaks her facade of middle-class respectability to enlist the aid of detectives to recover them. Mary does not "really feel alive without a feeling of guilt," and thus admits some responsibility. Grace, an admitted sinner, discreetly avoids overt injuries to others, recognizes her limitations, "happily conscious of the comparative innocence of her own past life." Whatever their own faults, each of these is free of solipsism.

Grace understands that human beings are not all the same; she is toughly realistic in her evaluation: "You're mistaken if you think wrong-doers are always unhappy. . . . The really professional evil-doers love it. . . . The pros are in their element." These remarks are made to Anthea, who represents in *Territorial Rights* the rigid, close hewing of the line. At the end of the interview with Mr. B., the nameless agent whose smiling face never alters, Anthea remarks, "Human nature is evil, isn't it?" Mr. B. notes, "I wouldn't call it evil.

Human nature is human nature as far as I'm concerned." The difficult question is how to cope with human nature.

If Robert's character is shown as evolving with no significant changes but only a clarification and intensification of his criminality, Curran also admits a sameness. He denies Violet's argument that during the war they were "different people . . . everything was different. Everyone else was different." Curran says, "We're the same people. . . . Any other point of view is foolish. We wouldn't be vulnerable if we were not the same people." Such sentiments of hopelessness are echoed in the extracts from the cheap popular novel that Anthea reads to distract herself from domestic difficulties. Spark's parody of the fiction that is never remembered is flawless. First relaxed by the process of inhalation, her character Matt says, "Well . . . I don't know." Later, amid the beer cans, he asks, "What choice is there, what choice ever, in the world of today?" He does nothing himself, and "after a long silence" says, "That's the way it is."

The takeover by those who deny territorial rights to others is one way of describing the mid-1970s, and Spark's two novels presented this reality. After using madness as a metaphor in early works of the decade, Spark worked toward a reexamination of human responsibility. The microcosm that she presented in Rome and Venice was filled with people whose lives are controlled by self-interest and immediate worldly concerns. However, there is an alternative, suggested by the splendid churches that stand as monuments to another age's belief and achievement. St. Mark's is not only an architectural masterpiece; it is a symbol of individual efforts united for a grand, larger whole: "the mosaics stood with the same patience that had gone into their formation, piece by small piece." Thus Spark announced that her next novel would be an exploration of how the artist creates.

11

Intense Detachment

Loitering with Intent

Loitering with Intent, nominated for the Booker-McConnell Prize for Fiction, is Spark's finest work in many years and provides an explicit statement about the relationship between art and life. Focusing on the writing of autobiography as well as the creation of a novel, Spark returns to the personal mode of her early works, but combines it with an extraordinary detachment. The novel presents an unmistakably Sparkian combination of peculiar characters, grotesques whose human frailties are exposed but also tolerated, even embraced as endearing, until they become solipsistic and thus menacing and dangerous. However, the satiric urgency of Spark's middle period was left behind in *Loitering with Intent*, and the evolving charity and acceptance of the later middle period are fully realized.

Spark's first novel, *The Comforters*, is about a woman writing a first novel and trying to justify the creation of fiction as a serious and appropriate endeavor. *Loitering with Intent* is about a successful novelist describing her creative life and reflecting upon the relation between autobiography and fiction. Through a manipulation of time sequence, the first-person protagonist recounts events from the crucial months during which she was completing her first novel; and she also interprets, after many years, what she was thinking and feeling in that formative period, as well as her mature reflections in the present.

As an analysis of the creative process and its relation to biography, *Loitering with Intent* is an apologia, an explanation, and a defense of the novelist's life. Spark presents not personal autobiography but an artist's life, describing the writer's process as it has been experienced and making critical judgments. Fiction and life are intermingled, but Spark clearly identifies the two as different. The "I" of the novel is Fleur Talbot, a fictional character but one whose experiences and style are identifiably Sparkian. She defines the role of the artist as the transfiguration of the commonplace: "What is truth? . . . When people say that nothing happens in their lives I believe them. But you must understand that everything happens to an artist; time is always redeemed, nothing is lost and wonders never cease." Receptivity distinguishes the artist from others, so that even the threatening and unpleasant can be entertained: "I was aware of a *daemon* inside me that rejoiced in seeing people as they were, and not only that, but more than ever as they were, and more, and more." Detachment like this is a far cry from the self-seeking that characterizes most lives. It is not an abnegation, but an intensification of response, though remarkably tolerant and accepting rather than insistent. The word "rejoiced" anticipates the refrain "I went on my way rejoicing" that describes Fleur's reaction to events throughout the novel.

Although it is a mature artist's reflections about her career, Fleur Talbot's story is largely an account of several months from the autumn of 1949 until the summer of 1950. She is very poor, living in a shabby bed-sitting room, writing, in London. She gratefully accepts a temporary job with Sir Quentin Oliver, who wants her to edit and type the work of the ten mem-

bers of the Autobiographical Association. These
memoirs are to be safely lodged for seventy years, to
avoid any possible libel of living persons, and then
given to posterity. Very much a snob, Sir Quentin
collects members of the Association, "men and women
of great distinction living full, very full lives." Nevertheless, they lack skill in writing, and the subject matter is impoverished, so that artistic development is
necessary.

Within the first week it occurs to Fleur that the
papers could easily be turned to blackmail—a
frequent theme in Spark's novels. Later Fleur understands how Sir Quentin is encouraging members of
the group to reveal themselves and insisting upon
"complete frankness." The members are all weak in
character, a "band of fools" easily "orchestrated." Sir
Quentin needles his authors and sometimes ad-
ministers Dexedrine; his dominance leads to destruction because the ruthless frankness and exposure
culminate in feelings of extreme guilt by all the members. Fleur thinks "complete frankness" is a mistake,
"a euphemism for rudeness"; she claims the artist's
detachment. But she also asserts that part of every artist's experience is a direct confrontation with evil.
Initially evil appears too incredible to seem real, but
then its truth is recognized. Fleur first suspects, and
then knows, that Sir Quentin is a lunatic. She confronts him and insists that the manipulation stop. After Sir Quentin is killed in a car accident, Fleur's
friend Dottie says that this event proves Fleur's novel
valid, since the fiction also has the hero die in a car
crash. Fleur bluntly distinguishes: "Nothing to do with
my *Warrender Chase*. Quite a different situation. The
man was pure evil." This is a judgment that separates
two realities, life and art; fiction is not the same thing
as living people.

At her first meeting with Triad Publishers, Fleur's
youthful work is praised: "The general consensus,"

said Leopold, "is that although the evil of Warrender is a shade over-accentuated, you have a universal theme. (Jump.)" The word "Jump" is significant, since both publisher and author "jumped"; Leopold decided to offer a contract, and Fleur accepted. Some readers loved the book, and others hated it. The mature Fleur reflects that early criticism of her novels as "exaggerated" is inaccurate, for what she presented were "merely aspects of realism."[1] Evil is not explained away; it is identified. This is most exactly discerned in the characters Warrender Chase/Sir Quentin Oliver.

To the novelist everything is important. Fleur's daytime work spills over into her nightly effort, which is the completion of a first novel. She explains that, long before she met Sir Quentin, she had conceived her hero Warrender Chase, whom her employer resembles remarkably. Indeed sometimes it is hard to distinguish whether life is imitating art or art imitating life. Warrender Chase is "privately a sado-puritan who for a kind of hobby gathered together a group of people specially selected for their weakness and folly, and in whom he carefully planted and nourished a sense of terrible and unreal guilt." The fictional character, who was suggested to her by a single overheard sentence, interestingly combines "public, formal High Churchism" and "a private sectarian style." Fleur is not concerned with his motives; she simply enjoys the fictional creation to which she brings energy. "Her sets of words convey ideas of worth and truth," and she enjoys the writing, thus rejecting the Romantic notion of the suffering artist. Fleur finds that details suggest themselves as needed. She describes the novelist as a "myth-maker" who understands "the work as a continuous poem," the wondrous work of one who can tell a story in countless ways.[2] However hard she works, Fleur never feels tired, for she is buoyed by the excitement of creation, and she even completes *Warrender Chase* during a case of flu.

The novelist's absorption seems absolute. Fleur's friend Wally tells her, "Sometimes when I'm with you, a very odd thing happens—you're suddenly not there. It's creepy." This habit of being somewhere else is suggested by the structure of *Loitering with Intent*; details of *Warrender Chase* alternate with the account of Fleur's connection with Sir Quentin's Autobiographical Association, and life and fiction intersect. Sir Quentin believes Fleur to be a "witch, an evil spirit who's been sent to bring ideas into his life." In fact, Sir Quentin, who is not an artist, is impoverished and appropriates Fleur's manuscript. He introduces chunks of her material into the autobiographies; he uses his influence to stop publication; and he arranges the theft of every copy of the manuscript. This is Sir Quentin's way of trying to absorb and destroy Fleur, for whom the novel is reality, a way of knowing and being. Unlike the suicide of Lady Bernice Gilbert, which Sir Quentin precipitates, the loss is not absolute because Fleur not only recovers the first novel, but also writes *All Souls' Day*, *The English Rose*, and others.

For all her absorption in the creative process, Fleur has a life with people who are not characters in her novel. She is a woman as well as an artist. Sensitive to others, she neither judges harshly nor exploits them. When she goes to work for Sir Quentin, she finds his mother, Lady Edwina, appealing. The old lady, who is looked after by a domineering housekeeper, Beryl Tims, likes Fleur. Sir Quentin and Tims treat the elderly woman—who reminds the reader of the characters in *Memento Mori*—like a child. They are embarrassed by her and try to keep her out of the way, even plying her with sleeping pills. Fleur finds Edwina attractive, for all her bizarre appearance, and loves her for her capacity to speak the truth. Edwina's mind is alert, and she bluntly rejects her son's arrogance and determination to control and exploit her. Even her incontinence, her "fluxive precipitations," is a response to mistreatment. Fleur enjoys Lady Edwina for what she is and behaves kindly. Others accuse Fleur of wanting an inheritance from the old lady, who is, in fact, penniless. Nevertheless, Edwina repays Fleur's kindness. She takes bits of Quentin's diary to provide Fleur with evidence, so that Fleur can both confront her employer with his theft of her novel and insist that he disband the group. After Quentin's death, Edwina survives for a happier period, paid for by her inheritance from the son, a "rotter" who wanted to gain her estate.

Fleur claims for herself a dual situation, one in life and one in art. Early in *Loitering with Intent*, she has a "most articulate" thought: "How wonderful it feels to be an artist and a woman in the twentieth century." The fact that Fleur is a woman and the conviction that she is a writer, converge "quite miraculously," and Fleur "goes on her way rejoicing." This last phrase comes from the *Autobiography* of Benvenuto Cellini and serves as the poetic refrain throughout the novel. The Italian Renaissance artist is "sheer magic" to her, with his enthusiasm and love of his art and craft, the contradictions in his life, and the wonder that he lived so richly. Simply stated, the artist's life is his acceptance of both good and misfortune. This is expressed in Cellini's confidence and eagerness: "By God's grace, I am now going on my way rejoicing."

The "robust and full-blooded" *La Vita* of Cellini is favored by Fleur as a model for autobiography, but she also admires and recommends to the Association John Henry Newman's *Apologia pro vita sua*. Fleur, a Roman Catholic like Spark, is also an expert on Newman. Life and fiction converge. Both Spark and Fleur were enormously influenced at the start of their careers by Newman, and each wrote about his life and work. Fleur admires Newman's sublimity and is attracted to the spiritual context. However, she reconsiders her appraisal when Maisie Young, one of the members of the Autobiographical Association to whom she gave it, singles out the passage in which Newman describes his boyhood religious feelings. He mistrusts material reality and rests in the thought, "two and two only supreme and luminously self-evident beings, myself and my Creator." Fleur cannot accept this limiting definition, she thinks it a "poetic vision only," "the expression of a nineteenth-century romantic," and she calls Newman's *Apologia* "a beautiful piece of poetic paranoia." This recalls Spark's long study of many Romantic writers, and her rejection of those who, like Jean Brodie, live a romantic vision.

Fleur insists that *everyone* is "a self-evident and luminous being"—even those who are not pleasing: "You can't live with an I-and-thou relationship to God and doubt the reality of the rest of life." She proves the sincerity of this sentiment in herself when she is happy to see Gray Mauser. As his name (dull, repeater) suggests, he is a "self-evident" person, hardly a character. But Fleur spends an evening with this awkward and anxious young poet, the homosexual lover of Leslie, her own on-again-off-again lover who is married to Dottie, also Fleur's friend, though the stealer of the manuscript. The relationships are tangled, but throughout Fleur is keen to make the best of whatever a human may be. She uses the experiences for her art, but she also deliberately treats everyone well. By disciplining herself (often with a prayer) away from any lack of sympathy, she genuinely enjoys whatever is. With such charity as the mode of her life, Fleur seems to have found a way between the extreme other-worldly religion of Newman and the sensuality of the artist Cellini.

When the Autobiographical Association is scheduled to move north, Dottie accuses Fleur of being able to forget too easily, and Fleur explains that this is not the case, because she will write about everything that has happened. Left alone, Fleur reads passages from both Newman's *Apologia* and Cellini's *Vita*, and she admires both. So different in other ways, the two are alike in recognizing their obligation to provide a true record. Newman wants to dispel the phantom views: "I wish to be known as a living man, and not as a scarecrow which is dressed up in my clothes." Cellini simply states that all "who have done anything of merit, or which verily have a semblance of merit, if so be they are men of truth and good repute, should write the tale of their life with their own hand."

Having forced the issue with Sir Quentin by presenting evidence of his theft of her novel and by pointing out that he must break up the Association and see a psychiatrist, Fleur is no longer responsible. Explicit comparison with Newman indicates the difference between Sir Quentin's "bunch of cranks" and the Oxford Anglo-Catholics at Littlemore. A "circle of devoted spiritual followers" for Sir Quentin is simply a reinforcement of his vanity and need to absorb others. Such evil is exposed and thus stopped. The man's death immediately after the confrontation symbolically suggests that evil can be destroyed when its existence is admitted. Fleur knows that Sir Quentin and his little sect are still a physical reality for her, but "they were morally outside" of herself, "objectified." Thus they can be dealt with by the detached artist.

Spark demonstrates the artist's method precisely with the opening and closing chapters of *Loitering with Intent*. Chapter One begins with a description of "one day in the middle of the twentieth century," when Fleur sits in an old graveyard in Kensington. She is writing a poem, and a young policeman comes over to talk. She does not recognize the significance of the day in her life, but is thinking that she needs a job, since she has recently escaped from the Autobiographical Association, and planning to continue her resistance to her landlord's attempts to get her to take a more expensive room. Chapter Twelve, the final one in the novel, begins with the same scene, but now its significance is explicit, and the description more detailed: "It was right in the middle of the twentieth century, the last day of June 1950, warm and sunny, a Friday, that I mark as a changing-point in my life." The young policeman saunters over, and Fleur asks what crime her sitting and writing could be considered. "Well, it could be desecrating and violating," he said, "it could be obstructing and hindering without due regard, it could be loitering with intent." As the title of the novel indicates, Spark clearly identifies the artist's crime as the last, though the other charges could and have been made against her novels. At the end of the chapter Fleur's friend Dottie, having read the large and favorable reviews of *Warrender Chase*, accuses Fleur of having "plotted and planned it all." Fleur agrees that she "had been loitering with intent." Spark's novel demonstrates how this behavior, the necessary prelude of creation, culminates in a novel. The language shows an assured verbal playfulness which gently masks basic laughter at human seriousness and foolishness.

Disconcertingly for some, Fleur—like many other Sparkian heroines—has the same kind of detachment about religious matters.[3] Her friend Dottie is a conventional Roman Catholic of 1950; Fleur's "concept of religion was of necessity different." Fleur is also

a Catholic believer but not that sort, not that sort at all. . . . I had an art to practice and a life to live, and faith abounding; and I simply didn't have the time or mentality for guilds and indulgences, fasts and feasts and observances. I've never held it right to create more difficulties in matters of religion than already exist.

On another later occasion, when Dottie dramatically announces that she has lost her faith, Fleur notes, "I was rather relieved since I had always

uneasily felt that if her faith was true then mine was
false." This delicate poise between contraries is like the
mystic's prayer, "Teach us to care and not to care."
Faith abounds in Fleur, who is never unaware of her
limited experience of reality. She acts morally in the
world, and she creates her art. She wants her novels to
give pleasure, but she accepts that some will give more
and some less.[4]

Loitering with Intent closes, like so many other
Spark novels, with a poetic image that provides the
essence of its argument. Fleur, the successful novelist,
lives in Paris, as does Dottie, who continues to have
problems and stress. Even though their experience
with the Autobiographical Association occurred thirty
years ago, Dottie still scolds Fleur, saying that she is
guilty of "wriggling out of real life," and Fleur is still
exasperated. She comes out into a courtyard where
small boys are playing football

and the ball came flying straight towards me. I kicked it
with a chance grace, which, if I had studied the affair and
tried hard, I never could have done. Away into the air it
went, and landed in the small boy's waiting hands. The boy
grinned. And so, having entered the fullness of my years,
from there by the grace of God I go on my way rejoicing.

Grace is not earned, it is a gift of God, but the woman
and the artist are ready, and joy is the result.

Understanding this religious context is crucial to an
appreciation of Spark's work, for it explains the
paradox of her apparent authorial omniscience and
real lack of seriousness in the ultimate sense. Fiction is
only the novelist's, not God's truth. Spark defined the
purpose of art as giving pleasure. She increasingly sim-
plified, for as Fleur learns, "how little one needs, in
the art of writing, to convey the lot, and how a lot of
words, on the other hand, can convey so little." In
early interviews, Spark said that she did very little
revising,[5] and Fleur explains why she does not change
her text: "I could see its defects as a novel but they

weren't the sort of defects that could be removed
without the entire essence . . . cosmetic treatment
won't serve." She always likes best the novel on which
she is working, so that *All Souls' Day*, then *The
English Rose* take over from *Warrender Chase*. Fleur
initially uses Dottie as a gauge for "the general
reader," but then agrees with Solly, her dearest friend
in the London years, that probably no such creature
exists. Fleur's final summary of her career and audience is: "It was a long time ago. I've been writing ever
since with great care. I always hope the readers of my
novels are of good quality. I wouldn't like to think of
anyone cheap reading my books." This is another
example of Spark's appeal, her flattering way of
making the reader believe that she is speaking directly
to him as an interested, intelligent, and educated
being with no need for the obvious statement. More
than thirty years of loitering with intent have
produced "a fullness from which by the grace of God
we go on our way rejoicing"—and wait eagerly for the
next novel, since we know that Spark is still loitering.

The Only Problem

Early in her career, in "The House of Fiction" interview of 1963, Spark explained her interest in truth.
Distinguishing several kinds of truth—metaphorical,
moral, anagogical, and absolute—she claimed that a
kind of truth emerged from her novels and identified
as most exacting "absolute truth, in which I believe
things which are difficult to believe, but I believe
them because they are absolute."[6] *The Only Problem*
comes nearer to absolute truth than any other work of
Muriel Spark. The epigraph of the novel is a line from
the book of Job 13:3:

Surely I would speak to the Almighty, and I desire to reason with God. Early in the narrative the hero explains that he is interested in discussing only one thing: "It is the only problem. The problem of suffering is the only problem. It all boils down to that."

The most exacting theological question has always been: How can God, Who is good, allow the suffering that makes life in this world so terrible? The difficulty of the question is heightened when the sufferer is good, a person innocent of wrongdoing. Central in the Judeo-Christian tradition is the Book of Job, which argues less about the mystery of suffering—that it is not a divine punishment for sins committed—than it probes the depths of faith in spite of suffering. Job is a man "simple and upright, and fearing God, and avoiding evil" (1:1). Yet his worldly possessions are taken away, and the three friends who come as comforters seem to offer more cruelty than consolation. Nevertheless, this book of the Old Testament shows that patience increases the worthiness of the sufferer, and then the glory of God is enhanced. Many exegetes have devoted themselves to Job, and Christian writers like Pope Gregory the Great (d. 608) have interpreted the text allegorically as an anticipation of the Passion of Christ the Redeemer.[7]

Spark's first novel, *The Comforters,* was deeply influenced by the Book of Job. In *The Only Problem* the mature novelist, as in *Loitering with Intent,* reexamines materials that were fundamental at the start of her career. Spark's 1955 review of Jung's interpretation is called "The Mystery of Job's Suffering," and *The Only Problem* almost exactly echoes her critical view that the comforters do not understand and that both the suffering and comforting are to be survived.[8] The novel's hero believes that Job's suffering is unending: "It became a habit, for he not only argued the problem of suffering, he suffered the problem of argument. And that is incurable." There is, then, a continuity in Spark's deliberations about suffering, but there are also significant differences. The only problem is unchanging, but as she reflects upon the mystery the novelist's attitude evolves from tension and hesitancy to calm and exaltation.

Harvey Gotham, a wealthy Canadian in his mid-thirties, lives alone in France, in St. Dié, a village in the district of Meurthe. Describing himself as studious, he wants peace of mind to do his work, which is to write a monograph on the Book of Job. This subject has been his consuming interest since he was a theological student when he identified Job as "the pivotal book of the Bible." The advantage of living in St. Dié is its proximity to Epinal, which he visits frequently to see Georges de la Tour's "sublime painting, *Job Visited by His Wife*."

The action of the novel spans approximately one year, and everything revolves around Harvey Gotham. A year earlier, while on holiday in Italy, he suddenly walked away from his wife Effie. Her gleeful announcement that she had stolen the two large chocolate bars they were eating had filled Harvey with dismay. Effie's explanation of her theft as an attack on the capitalist system overwhelmed Harvey, a character who is unable to recognize absurdity. Harvey, who describes himself as "studious," wants only to think about the Book of Job and to write a monograph explaining it. But, like his subject, Harvey is a rich man; and he is visited by comforters, various friends who come to France to expound their views about his situation—and to gain advantages for themselves.

The first to arrive, in April, is Edward Jansen, Harvey's brother-in-law and friend from their days as theological students. He is married to Effie's older sister Ruth, though he had long ago had an affair with the beautiful Effie. Ostensibly, Edward comes to argue Effie's wish for a divorce and settlement since she is pregnant by her current lover Ernie Howe. However, Edward wants some big change in his own life. He also needs money, since he has not yet established himself as an actor after giving up his life as a curate. Further, Edward resents Harvey's great wealth, intelligence, and detachment from everything except his work on Job.

The second visitor is Ruth, who brings Clara, Effie's baby born in June and left in her care. Ruth's original objective is to make Harvey balance accounts, but she finds herself very much at ease with Harvey and by October has settled in as his mistress and persuaded him to buy the local château. Having spent her childhood in a rectory, Ruth has lived a life in which "religion was her bread and butter." She is comfortable with a man whose attention is focused on understanding Scripture. Marriage to a curate was meaningful, but she is relieved to be free of Edward since she cannot tolerate living with an actor. The plainer sister, Ruth cares for Effie's child and appreciates Harvey's need for her presence. Harvey hardly notices the château, Ruth, or Clara; he works in the wretched cottage and often recognizes that he does not want people enough. However, he identifies Ruth as a "comforter"; she provides him with company and serves as analyst of his situation.

Two others come to the château. Nathan Fox is an unemployed graduate in English literature at the university where Ruth was teaching. He lives with Ruth and Edward, performs domestic tasks happily and ably, and dotes on the baby Clara. He comes to spend Christmas, bringing gifts and news of Effie's arrest in Trieste for shoplifting. The final visitor is Harvey's lawyer, Stewart Cowper, who comes to give advice after Effie is identified as part of a terrorist group, *Front de la Liberation de l'Europe*, that robs supermarkets, including one in Epinal. Soon afterwards Effie, whose battle name is Marion, is accused of killing a policeman in Paris. Since a British lawyer's professional use in France is limited, Stewart

rightly identifies himself: "I suppose I'm just a comforter."

Harvey is in need of comforting. Ruth takes Clara to
London for safety. The press descends upon him to
question him about Effie. After he appears on international television, his Auntie Pet telephones from
Canada to chide him for his religious statements. Harvey, of course, had used the press conference to talk
about Job. Anne-Marie, the daily help, is actually a
policewoman. But through all the unsettling
revelations about Effie, Harvey recognizes that he
loves his wife more than he had realized. When Auntie
Pet arrives from Toronto with evidence of Effie's
liaison with a young man in a California commune,
Harvey is skeptical about motives and questions this
view. Assertions about family honor do not touch him.
He bears yet more suffering and goes on with his
writing.

In the end Harvey is called to Paris for questioning
by two security men, Louis Pomfret and Chatelain,
and to identify the body of Effie, who was killed by
police when she opened fire in the eighteenth arron-
disement (Montmartre).

Having completed his monograph on Job after three
years, Harvey wonders whether Job was satisfied with
the plump reward of the Lord's blessing, increased
possessions, family, and years of life. At the end of
April, Edward returns to St. Dié to see Harvey and
bring news that Ernie Howe wants him to adopt
Clara, child of the terrorist Effie. Ruth, showing her
pregnancy, has returned with Clara, now a toddler.
Harvey answers Edward's question about what he will
do now that his work on Job is finished, by identifying
his future as an analogue to Job's: "Live another hundred and forty years. I'll have three daughters, Clara,
Jemima, and Eye-paint." Job had seven sons and three
daughters, Jemima (Dove), Keziah (Cinnamon) and
Kerenhappneh (Horn of eye-paint); and he lived one

hundred forty years in the Lord's blessing (42:12-17).

This conclusion expresses both calm acceptance and commitment to social responsibility. *The Only Problem* began with Harvey's retreat from his wife and friends; it concludes with a prospect of a long and full life with a wife and children. An observer of Harvey and his associates comments, "A lot can happen in a few months." What happens is a reconciliation to suffering, or perhaps the change is a recognition that preoccupation with suffering is not appropriate. One of Harvey's youthful, logical proposals in analyzing the Book of Job was that "the individual soul has made a pact with God before he is born, that he will suffer during his lifetime." He later recognizes that "Suffering isn't in proportion to what the sufferer deserves." This is reiterated just after he has heard about the policeman Effie was accused of killing: "We do not get what we merit. The one thing has nothing to do with the other. Your only course is to prevent it happening again." The addition in this statement is a crucial expression of hope, a belief that things can change and that human action makes a difference. At the police station in Epinal Harvey sees a man about whom he knows nothing except how he looks:

Patience, pallor and deep anxiety; there goes suffering, Harvey reflected. And I found him interesting. Is it only by recognizing how flat would be the world without the sufferings of others that we know how desperately becalmed our lives would be without suffering? Do I suffer on Effie's account? Yes, and perhaps I can live by that experience. We all need something to suffer about. But *Job*, my work on *Job*, all interrupted and neglected, probed into and interfered with: that is experience, too; real experience, not vicarious as is often assumed. To study, to think, is to live and suffer painfully.

This argues the universality of suffering and the difficulty of recognizing and defining it. Harvey's final point about Job and himself is: "I'm not even sure that

I suffer, I only endure distress. But why should I analyse myself? I am analysing the God of Job. . . . We are back to the Inscrutable. If the answers are valid then it is the questions that are cock-eyed." Quoting Job 38:2-3, Harvey notes "It is God who asks the questions in Job's book." In the last scene he no longer questions.

Spark's retelling of the story is based on the idea that "The *Book of Job* will never come clear. It doesn't matter; it's a poem." The reasoning asked for in the epigraph is unnecessary, even irrelevant. Georges de la Tour's painting of *Job Visited by His Wife* is a couple in their prime deeply in love, showing an idealized notion of the artist. Scriptural scholars also interpret and may continue to move about sections of the poem and argue dates of composition. None of this is as important as the presence of God to Job and Harvey. Pride about suffering, a need for self-vindication: both disappear in the presence of love. Harvey understands the Book of Job and loves Effie, though this is not reasonable. The Inscrutable needs no questions. Job/Harvey's "desire to reason with God" rightly wanes, for peace comes with the felt presence of God.

Such vigorous theology may seem intimidating in a novel, but Spark's wit and skill make this tale amusing and fascinating. As in *Memento Mori* she turns a potentially oppressive series of events and human responses into a lively and heartening experience. The theological argument is both significant and fully developed, but it is never overwhelming. Spark uses a simple technique of juxtaposing the comments on Job, always careful and thoughtful, with somewhat vague, casual, and brief references to the other events in Harvey's life. There is a fundamental absurdity in the student's preoccupation with his writing while his friends and wife are participating in a variety of sexual alliances, exploitation, and terrorist activities. There is also a fundamental absurdity in obsessive concern

with the things of this world and lack of attention to
eternity. As Gregory the Great's *Morals on the Book of
Job* explains, Job's (Harvey's) friends bewail his loss of
temporal prosperity. The ascetic basis of this explanation of Job is unfathomable in the twentieth century, but Harvey's avoidance of his great wealth is an
attempt to place himself in Job's situation. This is a
conscious seeking of the analagous experience. Living
poorly in the cottage helps Harvey to write his
monograph, and it also gives him the separation he
needs. He learns that Effie is much worse than he had
expected; she really is a terrorist, and killing a
policeman is very different from stealing a chocolate
bar. Effie's infidelities are more numerous and less
discriminating than he had expected. Nevertheless, he
loves her more. Love, of course, is no more rational
than human suffering; both simply are. When Harvey
recognizes this love in himself, he looks more kindly on
others. The unborn child and Clara—whose name
means light—offer a promise. Like other babies in
Spark's world, they are symbols of reaffirmation.

Early in the novel, before Harvey knows about
Effie's pregnancy, the idea of a baby is introduced. To
preserve his solitude at the cottage, Harvey hangs baby
clothes on the line and takes them in each day. His
assumption is that this will make people believe that
he is looked after and thus there will be few to interrupt him. He makes a joke to Edward that "the
police won't shoot if they believe a baby's inside." This
is prophetic; the police later suspect Harvey of being
involved in Effie's terrorism because of the ruse. The
interrogation scenes make much of it, but Harvey persists with his explanations of Job.

There is another similar absurd idea. Anne-Marie
leaves a lovely arrangement of flowers in an attempt to
comfort Harvey. He thinks that they are bugged and
tears the arrangement apart. Spark's use of and delight
in the matter of detective stories persists, and the

familiarity of this material gives credibility to the preoccupation with Job.

The most extraordinary scene, however, is Harvey's press conference. Sought out by the reporters who want to question him about Effie, Harvey agrees to meet journalists. With great energy he controls the event and turns it into a sustained commentary about the meaning of the Book of Job. When a tough pressman shouts that Harvey is there "to answer our questions," the reply is "Keep your voice down, please. The fact is that I am here because it is my home. You are here to listen to me. The subject is the *Book of Job* to which I have dedicated many years of my life." Harvey is relentless, and he continues with his "seminar on Job without pay." There is a glorious triumph here, for the insensitive and abusive newsmongers are utterly stopped by Harvey's singular preoccupation. His dedication to Job gives him the strength to resist their manipulations, and the press hear his news rather than make their own.

As in all of Spark's novels there are many amusing details. She slyly introduces phrases and ideas that are allusions to her previous novels; for example, "abounding faith" as in *Loitering with Intent*. This kind of playful joke is one of Spark's ways of flattering her audience. There are other curious statements that amuse: "August is a very boring month for everybody," or "We are looking for a political fanatic, not a bar of chocolate." There are several parodies of press releases that are both outrageously exaggerated, and thus funny, but also reminders that distortions are characteristically offered as truth because sensational effects sell and generate excitement.

Accounts in the popular press are often lurid, and this is an analogue to the negative qualities of Job's comforters. People seem to thrive on the sufferings of others, to be reassured because they can be sympathetic to difficulties, while feeling relief that they do not have the problems and can enjoy the comfort of being a comforter. One of Harvey's views is that Job's comforters do not come only to gloat; they also alleviate his nervous crisis by asking questions. This interpretation is supported by Harvey Gotham's personal experience. His chosen isolation from his family and friends is accomplished without the mental stress and nervous exhaustion of Spark's earlier protagonist Caroline Rose, in *The Comforters*. This first novel, also inspired by the Book of Job, is not peaceful, for Caroline constantly expresses her irritation with those around her and her anxiety about the Christian injunction to love. Perhaps because of his intelligence, "always ten thoughts ahead of everyone around him," Harvey does not love easily, but he is remarkably free of severe judgments against his acquaintances. Where Caroline Rose made many clever remarks, was preoccupied with her own state of mind and impatient with human limitations, Harvey is detached, almost unaware of self. He ignores his wealth, hardly notices those around him. He does not bewail or question his personal fate but thinks of the universal:

For he could not face that a benevolent Creator, one whose charming and delicious light descended and spread over the world, and being powerful everywhere, could condone the unspeakable sufferings of the world; that God did permit all suffering and was therefore, by logic of his omnipotence, the actual author of it, he was at a loss how to square with the existence of God, given the premise that God is good.

Harvey's retreat into an almost monastic situation to compose a monograph on the Book of Job is not permanent asceticism. Like Gregory the Great, the finest medieval commentator on the Scriptural text, Harvey must live in the active world. As a writer, Spark balances Harvey's precise, studious analysis of the pivotal text of the Bible with the bizarre and disturbing details of modern life in which instability of personal relations and acts of terrorism are commonplace.

Spark's speciality, of course, is "The Transfiguration of the Commonplace." In her two latest novels she returns to the precise subject matter of her first novel, *The Comforters. Loitering with Intent* reexamines the making of the artist; *The Only Problem* reexamines the making of faith. These two novels, like the romance plays of Shakespeare, are the work of a remarkable maturity. The only problem, human suffering, has not and will not change. What has changed through the work of Spark is her capacity first to articulate the problem with increasing clarity, and then to show that the reasoning of the problem is a human preoccupation that torments those who believe in God.

12

The Comic Vision of
Muriel Spark

Muriel Spark has frequently stated her "generalized conclusion that the purpose of art is to give pleasure,"[1] and reviewers have most often praised her humor and fun. Thus any critic must feel uneasy about too earnest and labored an interpretation of the work of Muriel Spark.[2] She almost certainly does not take it as seriously as the critic does: every novel has an element of game or at least wry reflection. But Spark also explained that much of her life and writing was "based on the nevertheless idea." Even a statement of unmitigated fact required qualification. The word "nevertheless" best described her experiences when she was growing up in Edinburgh, and she "was fairly indoctrinated by the habit of thought which calls for this word."[3] My reading of Spark's work and this conclusion are made, then, with a Sparkian expectation that there is always a "nevertheless" response.

Combined with statements that the purpose of art is to give pleasure are Spark's avowals that art is also a way of informing, even a kind of propaganda, "since it propagates a point of view and provokes a response."[4] In her lecture before the American Academy of Arts and Letters, Spark further declared that "the art of literature is a personal expression of ideas which come to influence the minds of people even at second, third, and fourth hand."[5] Confident that "even the simplest, the least sophisticated and uneducated mind" is aware of the moment in which we live as a time when "we are surrounded on all sides and oppressed by the absurd," Spark opposed the idea that literature was intended for "a sophisticated minority."[6] Her plea was for the "desegregation of art," "the liberation of our minds from the comfortable calls of lofty sentiment in which they are confined and never really satisfied."[7] Her concomitant favoring of satirical writing—"Ridicule is the only honorable weapon we have left"[8]—may have reflected the intensity of social protest that characterized the time, but the essential sentiments have been consistent throughout Spark's work. Her view of the artist was neatly summarized in a question she posed to interviewer Philip Toynbee: "Don't you think as writers our job is to bring about an environment of honesty and self-knowledge, a sense of the absurd and a general looking-lively to defend ourselves from the ridiculous oppression of our time? And above all to entertain our readers in the process."[9] Asked whether she wanted to make any public impact, Spark replied to a 1961 interviewer, "In all four fields [political, moral, spiritual, intellectual] I would like more readers to see things as I do, because the more readers I have the less lonely a mind I feel."[10] Clearly she has been a very serious writer, one who saw art as directly related to life, though not the same thing as life.

Spark's view of the dual purpose of literature embodies the classical precepts epitomized by the Roman poet Horace in the words *docere* ("to teach") and *delectare* ("to delight"). Perhaps it also explains why Spark chose the form of the short novel for her major work. Believing that the art of rhetoric or persuasion had the greatest potential for influence, she noted that "the short novel stands as good a chance as any other art form of infiltrating the public mind."[11] Statements like these place her firmly in the great moral tradition of British literature. This is a view that literature not only gives pleasure, but also is concerned with values, and it is not the prevailing contemporary view that stresses aesthetics. Spark's exploitation of humor is partially an attempt to make more palatable her serious intentions. Sometimes it is shockingly grim, but most often it is bright, a comic view that mitigates, one suspects, both her own dark perceptions and the audience's.

Perhaps the most consistent quality of Spark's writing is the poetic style. Unsurpassed for its simplicity, spareness, and exquisite employment of extraordinarily vivid images, it is the more remarkable because the actual words are short and easily understood, yet the resonances of meaning are many. The dialogue sounds convincingly authentic, but each voice is refined through Spark's poetic control. The effects might be described as mannered, but they are not, because there is no self-indulgence or authorial imposition.

This is possible because, as John Updike observed, "detachment is the genius of her fiction."[12] Even in the most satiric passages Spark remains dispassionate. She does not allow herself the easier emotional appeals, but consistently presents a challenge that makes her audience think. The leanness and coolness of narrative and style preserve a distance. With Spark this is more than the traditional achievement of British fiction recognized by Updike as "a certain dispassionate elevation above the human scene" and characterized by "greater gaiety, ease of contrivance, superior finish." It is a comic vision for which one must look back to a medieval Christian writer like Dante or Chaucer to find a comparison.

Early in her career, Spark reviewed C. J. Jung's study of the Book of Job, the scriptural text which also informed her first novel, *The Comforters*, and the most recent, *The Only Problem*. She analyzed the Epilogue of Job, a "happy ending" that Jung ignored, as "anagogical humour which transcends irony and which is infinitely mysterious." She suggested that the

ending was not merely conventional but offered
something that the upright Job had to acquire, "some
wisdom which combines heavenly ideas with earthly
things."[13] Further, Spark admired Proust, "agnostic,
hedonist, self-centered neurotic," for a similar reason:
"He reminds us that there is a method of apprehending
eternity through our senses, analogous to our
sacramental understanding of eternity by faith."[14]
Though there is, even among contemporary
Christians, less evidence of it now, this combination of
temporal with eternal persisted in Spark's thought and
belief. It is on this basis that she introduced Newman
and Cellini as the two most admired writers of
autobiography in *Loitering with Intent*.

Spark's biography and comments provide evidence
of an unusually sensitive person, subject to grave
psychological and emotional disorders, but fiercely
determined and disciplined. She describes herself as
touched by "the puritanical strain of the Edinburgh
ethos."[15] Significantly, she does not view the
puritanical virtues, like industriousness or reticence
about sex, negatively. Nevertheless, she observed,
"spiritual joy does not come in an easy consistent flow
to the puritanically-nurtured soul. Myself, I have had
to put up a psychological fight for my spiritual joy."[16]
The novels, I think, record that fight and provide us
with a remarkable personal and artistic achievement.

Muriel Spark has been eager to please, to provoke
laughter, and to rise above the human scene to a point
of disinterestedness. She has shown the self-controlled
poise of an intellectual pessimist in her stark
delineation of human beings, but this has been combined with the emotional optimism that comes from
"faith abounding" and a commitment to fellowship
and charity in the world. The combination is an extraordinary one, and Spark's talent has greatly
enriched twentieth-century fiction; it has also
provided an antidote to spiritual dryness.

Notes

Chapter 1

1. Spark, Muriel. "The First Year of My Life." *The Times Saturday Review*, Dec. 13, 1975, p. 8.
2. Spark, Muriel. "What Images Return." *Memoirs of a Modern Scotland*, ed. Karl Miller (London: Faber and Faber, 1970), p. 151.
3. Kermode, Frank. "The House of Fiction." *Partisan Review*, Vol. XXX (Spring 1963), p. 79.
4. Spark, Muriel. "My Conversion." *Twentieth Century*, Vol. CLXX, No. 1011 (Autumn 1961), p. 62.
5. Howard, Elizabeth Jane. "Writers in the Tense Present." *The Queen*, Centenary Issue, 1861–1961 (Aug. 1961), p. 146.
6. Kemp, Peter. *Muriel Spark* (London: Peter Elek, 1974), pp. 9-10.
7. Spark, Muriel. "The Religion of an Agnostic." *The Church of England Newspaper*, Nov. 27, 1953, p. 1.
8. Spark, "My Conversion," p. 60.
9. Kermode, "The House of Fiction," p. 79.
10. Ibid., pp. 80–81.
11. Scroggie, Jean. "Mementos for Muriel Spark." *The Daily Telegraph*, Sept. 25, 1970, p 15.
12. Massie, Allan. *Muriel Spark* (Edinburgh: The Ramsay Head Press, 1979), p. 24.
13. Spark, Muriel. "How I Became a Novelist." *John O'London's*, Vol. 3, No. 61 (Dec. 1960), p. 683.
14. Kemp, *Muriel Spark*, p. 71.
15. Holland, Mary. "The Prime of Muriel Spark." *The Observer* Colour Magazine, Oct. 17, 1965, p. 10.
16. *Proceedings of the American Academy of Arts and Letters*. New York: American Academy of Arts and Letters, 1971, p. 25.

Chapter 2

1. Spark, "What Images Return," p. 151.
2. Spark, Muriel. "Keeping It Short." *The Listener*, Sept. 24, 1970, p. 411.
3. Kemp, *Muriel Spark*, pp. 71–73.
4. The French Protestant theologian John Calvin (1509–1564) completed the *Institutes of the Christian Religion* in 1536 in Geneva, where austere reforms were later implemented. Civic authorities were responsible for enforcing religious teaching, and all areas of life were regulated. In Scotland John Knox was the advocate of this theology, and in the colonial United States Jonathan Edwards introduced a modified version. Intense biblicism and resolute theocentricity, magnifying the sovereignty and providence of God, are fundamental in Calvinism, which is thus strongly related to the theology of St. Augustine (354–430), the most influential writer in the early period of the Catholic Church. A distinction of Calvinism is that it bridges the gulf between the luxury of the world and the life of the spirit by dedicating them to the service of God. This quality was strongly appealing in an age of expanding capitalism.
5. Lodge, David. "The Uses and Abuses of Omniscience: Method and Meaning in Muriel Spark's *The Prime of Miss Jean Brodie*." *The Novelist at the Crossroads* (Ithaca, New York: Cornell University Press, 1971), pp. 143–44.
6. Gibson, John S. *Deacon Brodie Father to Jekyll and Hyde* (Edinburgh: Paul Harris, 1977).

Chapter 3

1. Kermode, "The House of Fiction," p. 79.
2. Spark, Muriel. "The Mystery of Job's Suffering: Jung's New Interpretation Examined." *The Church of England Newspaper*, Apr. 15, 1955, p. 7.
3. Ohmann, Carol B. "Muriel Spark's *Robinson*." *Critique*, Vol. VIII (1965), pp. 70–84.

Chapter 4

1. Boase, T. S. R. *Death in the Middle Ages Mortality, Judgment and Remembrance* (London: Thames and Hudson, 1972), provides an elementary survey and many illustrations of artistic representations.

2. Ariès, Philippe. *Western Attitudes toward Death*, trans. Patricia M. Ranum (Baltimore: Johns Hopkins University Press, 1974), and *The Hour of Our Death*, trans. Helen Weaver (New York: Alfred A. Knopf, 1981). The latter is interestingly reviewed by Paul Robinson, "Five Models for Dying," *Psychology Today*, March 1981, pp. 85–91.

Chapter 5

1. Spark had her own office at *The New Yorker*. After three years in America, she left because, "I found I simply couldn't stand the party line—I mean the way there was always a right and approved reaction to every situation." See Interview with Toynbee, *The Observer*, Nov. 7, 1971, p. 73.
2. Children in England are given an examination at eleven-plus years to determine whether they should prepare for university or leave school after completing the School Certificate.

Chapter 6

1. Spark, "How I Became a Novelist," p. 683.
2. Kermode, "The House of Fiction," p. 79.
3. This statement is almost exactly Spark's own in "My Conversion," p. 60: "But I never think of myself as a Catholic when I'm writing because it's so difficult to think of myself as anything else. It's all instinctive."

Chapter 7

1. Holland, "The Prime of Muriel Spark," p. 10.
2. The mixture of religions is close to Spark's own, though her father was Jewish and her mother Christian. There are also parallels in Barbara's conversion.
3. A convenient modern translation is *The Cloud of Unknowing* (New York: Penguin Books, 1961), by Clifton Wolters.
4. Spark named Alain Robbe-Grillet as a contemporary novelist much admired. Philip Toynbee Interview in *The Observer* Colour Magazine, November 7, 1971, p. 73. She had been "keen" about him as early as "Writers in the Tense Present," 1961, p. 146.
5. Spark later thought that the beginning was slow and the end very rapid. "Keeping It Short," p. 412.

Chapter 8

1. Spark explained in the Interview with Toynbee (*Observer*, 1971, p. 73): "But I don't read many novels. I love the glossies and the newspapers and film mags; and that's where I find a lot of my material."
2. *The Public Image* is a first reflection of Spark's life in Rome as a rich and famous author.
3. Spark, "Keeping It Short," p. 412.
4. Houts, Marshall. *They Asked for Death* (New York: Cowles, 1971), contains case histories of persons who deliberately goaded someone into murdering them and comments from psychiatric specialists.
5. Waugh, Auberon. "Review of *Not to Disturb*," *The Spectator*, Nov. 20, 1971, p. 733.
6. Toynbee Interview, 1971, p. 74. This reiterates Spark's view in "The Desegregation of Art," 1971.
7. Barbara Vaughan quotes the relevant passage, Apocalypse, Chapter 3, versus 15–16, to Freddy Hamilton in *The Mandelbaum Gate*.
8. Toynbee Interview, 1971, p. 74.

Chapter 9

1. Holland, "The Prime of Muriel Spark," p. 9.
2. This echoes a point in Spark, "The Desegregation of Art," 1971, p. 26.
3. Harper, Ralph. *The World of the Thriller* (Cleveland: Case Western Reserve University, 1969).
4. Associated Press Story, *The Berkeley Gazette*, Feb. 7, 1975, p. 1. Spark's fascination with "how Watergate blew up from nothing" reflects her earlier perspective, "I can never now suffer from a shattered faith in politics and politicians, because I never had any." "What Images Return," p. 153.

Chapter 10

1. Spark spends part of her time at a small holiday place at Nemi. Glendinning, Victoria. "Talk with Muriel Spark," *The New York Times Book Review*, May 20, 1970, p. 47.
2. Sculptural representations are of a figure covered with pendant fruits.

Chapter 11

1. Spark argued for this quality in the Toynbee Interview, 1971, p. 74. "I'm tremendously against the kind of literature which is making a constant appeal to our emotional sympathy." She compared life and art in "Keeping It Short," p. 412: "I like purple passages in my life, I like drama. But not in my writing. I think it's bad manners to inflict a lot of emotional involvement on the reader—much nicer to make them laugh and to keep it short."
2. Spark explained: "Things just happen and one records what has happened a few seconds later. . . . I do know that events occur in my mind and I record them. Whether it fits in with this theory, that theory, this myth, that myth, has nothing to do with me." Kermode, "The House of Fiction," p. 81.
3. Spark's explanation about why she became a Catholic is typical: "I couldn't believe anything else. It didn't particularly appeal to me: it still doesn't, but I'm still a Catholic. If I could believe anything else, I would." "Keeping It Short," p. 412.
4. Spark frequently stressed the significance of pleasure. "My whole aim, and I think the whole aim of art, is to give pleasure in one way or another." "Keeping It Short," p. 412.
5. Spark, "How I Became a Novelist," p. 683; Holland, "The Prime of Muriel Spark," p. 9.
6. Kermode, "The House of Fiction," pp. 80-81. See the full quotation in Chapter 1, p. 9.
7. *Morals on the Book of Job by S. Gregory the Great*, trans. J. Bliss, 3 vols. in 4 (London: J. H. Parker, 1844–50 [A Library of the Fathers of the Holy Catholic Church, vols. 18, 21, 22, 31]).
8. Spark, "The Mystery of Job's Suffering: Jung's New Interpretation Examined," p. 7.

Chapter 12

1. Spark, "The Desegregation of Art," p. 25.
2. Spark declared, "I'm always fascinated by what people see in them, much more than I ever knew I wrote." "The Prime of Muriel Spark," p. 10.
3. Spark, "What Images Return," p. 152.
4. Spark, "The Desegregation of Art," p. 25.
5. Ibid., p. 22.

6. Ibid., p. 26.
7. Ibid., p. 26.
8. Ibid., p. 24.
9. Spark in Toynbee Interview, p. 74.
10. Howard, "Writers in the Tense Present," p. 143.
11. Ibid., p. 145.
12. Updike, John. "Creatures of the Air." *The New Yorker*, Sept. 30, 1961, p. 161.
13. Spark, "The Mystery of Job's Suffering," p. 7.
14. Spark, "The Religion of an Agnostic," p. 1.
15. Spark, "What Images Return," p. 153.
16. Ibid., p. 153.

Bibliography

1. Writings of Muriel Spark

Critical Books

Tribute to Wordsworth. Ed. With Derek Stanford. London: Allan Wingate, 1950.

Child of Light: A Reassessment of Mary Wollstonecraft Shelley. Hadleigh, Essex: Tower Bridge Publications, 1951.

A Selection of Poems by Emily Brontë. London: Grey Walls Press, 1952.

Emily Brontë: Her Life and Work. With Derek Stanford. London: Peter Owen, 1953.

John Masefield. London: Peter Nevill, 1953.

My Best Mary. Selected Letters of Mary Wollstonecraft Shelley. Ed. with Derek Stanford. London: Allan Wingate, 1953.

The Brontë Letters. Selected. London: Peter Nevill, 1954.

Letters of John Henry Newman. A selection. Ed. with Derek Stanford. London: Peter Owen, 1957.

Poems

The Fanfarlo and Other Verse. Aldington, Kent: Hand and Flower Press, 1952.

Collected Poems I. London: Macmillan, 1970.

Going up to Sotheby's. London: Granada, 1982.

Plays

Voices at Play. Philadelphia: J. B. Lippincott, 1961.

Doctors of Philosophy. London: Macmillan, 1963. New York: Alfred A. Knopf, 1966.

Short Stories

The Go-Away Bird and Other Stories: London: Macmillan, 1958. Philadelphia: J. B. Lippincott, 1960.
Voices at Play (including Radio Plays). London: Macmillan, 1961. Philadelphia: J. B. Lippincott, 1961.
Collected Stories I. London: Macmillan, 1967. Alfred A. Knopf, 1968.

Children's Book

The Very Fine Clock. London: Macmillan, 1969. New York: Alfred A. Knopf, 1969.

Novels

The Comforters. London: Macmillian, 1957. Philadephia: J. B. Lippincott, 1957.
Robinson. London: Macmillan, 1958. Philadelphia: J. B. Lippincott, 1958.
Memento Mori. London: Macmillan, 1959. Philadelphia: J. B. Lippincott, 1959.
The Ballad of Peckham Rye. London: Macmillan, 1960. Philadelphia: J. B. Lippincott, 1960.
The Bachelors. London: Macmillan, 1960. Philadelphia: J. B. Lippincott, 1961.
The Prime of Miss Jean Brodie. London: Macmillan, 1961. Philadelphia: J. B. Lippincott, 1962.
The Girls of Slender Means. London: Macmillan, 1963. New York: Alfred A. Knopf, 1963.
The Mandelbaum Gate. London: Macmillan, 1965. New York: Alfred A. Knopf, 1965.
The Public Image. London: Macmillan, 1968. New York: Alfred A. Knopf, 1968.
The Driver's Seat. London: Macmillan, 1970. New York: Alfred A. Knopf, 1970.
Not to Disturb. London: Macmillan, 1971. New York: Alfred A. Knopf, 1971.
The Hothouse by the East River. London: Macmillan, 1973. New York: Viking, 1973.

The Abbess of Crewe. London: Macmillan, 1974. New York: Viking, 1974.

The Takeover. London: Macmillan, 1976. New York: Viking, 1976.

Territorial Rights. London: Macmillan, 1979. New York: Coward, McCann and Geoghegan, 1979.

Loitering with Intent. London: Macmillan, 1981. New York: Coward, McCann and Geoghegan, 1981.

The Only Problem. London: Macmillan, 1984. New York: G. P. Putnam's Sons, 1984.

Articles and Interviews with Muriel Spark

"The Desegregation of Art." Proceedings of the American Academy of Arts and Letters and the National Institute of Arts and Letters. New York, 1971.

"The First Year of My Life." *The Times Saturday Review*, Dec. 13, 1975.

"The House of Fiction." Interview with Frank Kermode. *Partisan Review*, Vol. XXX (1963)

"How I Became a Novelist." *John O'London's*, Dec. 1, 1960.

"Keeping It Short." Interview with Ian Gillham. *The Listener*, Sept. 24, 1970.

"Mementos for Muriel Spark." Interview with Jean Scroggie. *The Daily Telegraph*, Sept. 25, 1970.

"My Conversion." *Twentieth Century*, Vol. CLXX, No. 1011 (Autumn 1961).

"The Mystery of Job's Suffering: Jung's New Interpretation Examined." *The Church of England Newspaper*, April 15, 1955.

"The Prime of Muriel Spark." Interview with Mary Holland. *The Observer* Colour Magazine, Oct. 17, 1965.

"The Religion of an Agnostic." *The Church of England Newspaper*, Nov. 27, 1953.

"Talk with Muriel Spark." Interview with Victoria Glendinning. *The New York Times Book Review*, May 20, 1979.

"Twenty Years After." Interview with Philip Toynbee. *The Observer* Colour Magazine, Nov. 7, 1971.

"What Images Return," in Miller, Karl, ed., *Memoirs of a Modern Scotland*. London: Faber and Faber, 1970.

"Writers in the Tense Present." Interview with Elizabeth Jane Howard. *The Queen*, Centenary Issue (Aug., 1961).

2. Books and Monographs about Muriel Spark

Kemp, Peter. *Muriel Spark*. London: Paul Elek, 1974.
Malkoff, Karl. *Muriel Spark*. New York: Columbia University Press, 1968.
Massie, Allan. *Muriel Spark*. Edinburgh: The Ramsay Head Press, 1979.
Stanford, Derek. *Muriel Spark: A Biographical and Critical Study*. Fontwell: Centaur Press, 1963.
Stubbs, Patricia. *Muriel Spark*. Harlow, Essex: Longmans for the British Council, 1973.
Whittaker, Ruth. *The Faith and Fiction of Muriel Spark*. New York: St. Martin's Press, 1982.

3. Articles on Muriel Spark

Bradbury, Malcolm. "Muriel Spark's Fingernails." In Spacks, Patricia Meyer, editor, *Contemporary Women Novelists*. Englewood Cliffs, New Jersey: Prentice-Hall, 1977.
Duffy, Martha. "Review of *The Driver's Seat.*" *Time*, Oct. 26, 1970.
Harrison, Barbara Grizzuti. "Review of *Loitering with Intent.*" *The New York Times Book Review*, May 31, 1981.
Hart, Francis Russell. *The Scottish Novel from Smollett to Spark*. Cambridge: Harvard University Press, 1978.
Hoyt, Charles Alva. "Muriel Spark: The Surrealist Jane Austen." In Shapiro, Charles, *Contemporary British Novelists*. Carbondale and Edwardsville: Southern Illinois University Press, 1969.
Hynes, Samuel. "The Prime of Miss Muriel Spark." *Commonweal*, Feb. 23, 1962.
Karl, Frederick. "Muriel Spark." *The Contemporary English Novel*. New York: Farrar, Straus, and Giroux, 1972, rev. ed.
Kermode, Frank. "The Prime of Miss Muriel Spark." *New Statesman*, Sept. 27, 1963.
Kermode, Frank. "The Novel as Jerusalem: Muriel Spark's *The Mandelbaum Gate.*" *Continuities*. London: Routledge and Kegan Paul, 1968.

Kermode, Frank. "Review of *The Driver's Seat.*" *The Listener*, Sept. 24, 1970.

Kermode, Frank. "Review of *Not to Disturb.*" *The Listener*, Nov. 11, 1971.

Kermode, Frank. "Review of *The Takeover.*" *New Statesman*, June 4, 1976.

Lodge, David. "The Uses and Abuses of Omniscience: Method and Meaning in Muriel Spark's *The Prime of Miss Jean Brodie.*" *The Novelist at the Cross Roads.* Ithaca, New York: Cornell University Press, 1971.

Malin, Irving. "The Deceptions of Muriel Spark." In Friedman, Melvin J., *The Vision Obscured.* New York: Fordham University Press, 1970.

May, Derwent. "Review of *The Hothouse by the East River.*" *The Listener*, March 1, 1973.

Ohmann, Carol B. "Muriel Spark's *Robinson.*" *Critique*, Vol. VIII (1965).

Potter, Nancy A. J. "Muriel Spark: Transformer of the Commonplace." *Renascence*, Vol. XVII (1965).

Richmond, Velma Bourgeois. "The Darkening Vision of Muriel Spark." *Critique*, Vol. XV (1973).

Schneider, Harold W. "A Writer in Her Prime: The Fiction of Muriel Spark." *Critique*, Vol. V (1962).

Stanford, Derek. *Inside the Forties.* London: Sidgwick and Jackson, 1977.

Waugh, Auberon. "Review of *Collected Stories I* and *Collected Poems I.*" *The Spectator*, Dec. 12, 1967.

Wildman, John. "Translated by Muriel Spark." In Stanford, Donald E., ed. *Nine Essays in Modern Literature.* Baton Rouge: Louisiana State University Press, 1965.

Wilson, A. N. "Review of *Loitering with Intent.*" *The Spectator*, May 23, 1981.

Wood, Michael. "Review of *The Takeover.*" *The New York Review of Books*, Nov. 11, 1976.

Updike, John. "Creatures of the Air." *The New Yorker*, Sept. 30, 1961.

Index

193